SELF-PUBLISHING
FOR THE FREELANCE

SELF-PUBLISHING
FOR THE FREELANCE

Nik Chmiel

 BFP BOOKS London

A catalogue record for this book is available from the British Library

ISBN 0-907297-37-4

Published by BFP Books, Focus House, 497 Green Lanes, London N13 4BP.
Printed in Hong Kong.

To Tansy, who gave me support and encouragement when I needed it

Contents

Introduction   9

1. Getting Started   11

2. Images   22

3. Production   42

4. Marketing   60

5. Selling   86

6. Art Publishing   104

7. Business Matters   116

Further Reading   138

Index   139

Introduction

This book is about self-publishing for the freelance image-maker. It is written with the photographer in mind, but any creator of visual art, wishing to reproduce their work in other ways and sell it, should benefit from reading it.

The focus of the book is on small-scale self-publishing enterprises, but there are pointers to growing bigger. In particular the chapters on marketing and business matters contain information relevant to many different sizes of business. I also discuss the pros and cons of different forms of financing a business.

I am primarily concerned here with postcard, greetings card and poster self-publishing. I will also deal with books and with fine art products such as photographic prints. Some of these activities are more viable than others on a limited budget, but there is a serious lack of good individual products in the marketplace. The major publishers produce and sell in huge quantities, and tend to be very conservative. They have to be to sell to the widest audience. Thus there is a place for you, if you are willing to be adventurous.

The most important question you have to ask yourself is why do you want to self-publish? Why do you have the desire to create, design, produce, market, sell and distribute your imagery?

This question is important because self-publishing means lots of hard work and frustration, often with little or no financial reward. Are you prepared for this, or would you be better off taking your imagery to others who will do the publishing for you?

There are all sorts of reasons why you may be thinking of doing it yourself. Included among them are that no-one else will publish your images; that you have a strong belief in your own artistic vision and want your own artistic control; that what you have is unique and would be lost in a bigger product line; that your projected business is too small for major publishers; that you want to start a business, or to expand or diversify an existing business; that you want to take a step towards a different field; or that you may want to promote other crafts, for example paintings, sculpture or ceramics.

These reasons need to be sorted out because they will affect the goals you set for yourself and the way you do business. For example, if you have a set of strong, individual images you believe in, and you have a vision in your mind of each one as a finished poster, with your name at the bottom, ask yourself why you want them published, and why you are prepared to take the financial risk and endure the hard graft of doing the publishing yourself.

If the answer is simply to see your work in print, or adorning walls, you will be satisfied with no profit, and you will choose only the images you are proudest of for reproduction. On the other hand, if your motive is a successful business, with good profits on the back of satisfying images, then you will choose pictures which meet a market demand and sell well. Reproduction values will be selected according to popular taste and profit margins.

Of course, a combination of these two extremes is probably desired in the majority of cases. After all, why are you creating images in the first place if not to realise some artistic talent?

Nonetheless it pays to be realistic at the beginning in order to avoid disappointment later. It is easy to delude oneself, as almost any creative person will know. Photographers and artists are very often their own worst editors.

A key question is whether other publishers have refused to produce your work. If you have approached them and been rejected, you should ask yourself why. Is it that the imagery is no good, or does it just not fit in with their marketing position and strategy? Be honest with yourself. If you aren't, you will be the one to lose.

Another thing to bear in mind is that self-publishing also requires skills in design, production, marketing, selling and distributing your product. Are you able in these areas, or will you need to buy in expertise? The latter can prove expensive and make your venture financially precarious.

At the outset you may not know the answers to some of these questions. This book aims to raise these issues and explore them in some detail in order to prepare you for potential pitfalls and side alleys. Keep the points made during the course of the book in mind, and think about what you can and cannot do. Again, be realistic.

In the end you may decide to have a go. Well done! You have lots of work ahead of you, and a large degree of uncertainty, but the rewards can be worth it. It is a thrill to see your images in print, and to find that the public like them enough to buy them. You may even find that you can earn money as well!

1 Getting Started

This chapter is concerned with the transition from an image idea to the process of self-publishing. It is about those factors connected with any self-publishing venture which need to be considered at the outset. Thus it tempers dreams with a realistic edge.

More detailed treatment of many of the issues raised here are to be found in later chapters in this book; this chapter is focused on making you aware of the range of factors to bring to mind when contemplating self-publishing.

First steps

The transition from day-dreaming about the brilliant pictures you've produced, or are going to produce, to deciding what you are going to do with them, is the foundation of your future in self-publishing. This is not an easy step to take, and so it is worth putting time aside to think through what you are trying to achieve.

Are you an advanced amateur, producing good pictures which give you pleasure, and perhaps entering the odd competition hoping to win one of the big prizes? Have you built up a large body of work which family and friends have consistently praised, urging you to make some money out of them? Or are you already an experienced freelance, with a stock of images that you are regularly selling to various outlets?

Or are you, better still, a person with no existing saleable images, but someone with good skills sure that you could do better than the material currently published?

Why better still? Because it means you can decide what you are trying to achieve, and then set out to achieve it. The difference between this course of action and that of attempting to fit pictures you have already produced into the market is huge. It is a completely different way of thinking about your activities. It is important to ponder this difference.

If you try to fit existing pictures into a market then the likelihood is you will end up with a product range which looks incoherent. There will be no theme or common thread running through the images.

For example, your best photographs may be of a variety of subjects taken in your locality. You have a stunning shot of the Town Hall which you just know will make a superb postcard. The picture was taken in beautiful light early one morning. There are no people in it, and the sun is glinting off the windows, giving the whole image a sparkle. You have underexposed the shot to give a dark-toned, moody atmosphere.

Your next best image is a great shot of the local market. The day was overcast when you took it, but the colours in the market dominate the picture and the people in it are really interesting. This too could be a postcard.

However, if you market both these two pictures in the same range it will appear fragmented. It may be far better to separate these images into different ranges or produce them as one-offs. The point is that you are not just selling images, you are marketing a product. This means you need to think "long term" about your aims and objectives.

One of the most important steps to take when getting started, therefore, is to plan what you want to do and achieve. Thus you will have to think clearly and set goals. By doing this you can get a good idea of what stages you need to go through in order to bring your product to market, what that market is, and where you want to be in it.

Size matters

One of the first questions should be how big or small you want your operation to be. In other words what kind of outlay are you going to have to consider in order to get started. This initial decision affects all kinds of subsequent choices and so is worth lots of thought.

"Small is beautiful" could be your best motto if you have no prior experience of the publishing market you are about to enter. After all, what you do well is take photographs – you may or may not have other skills which could make the difference between success and failure. Therefore your first venture will certainly have a large element of learning in it, and business conditions may conspire to bring about failure before you've learnt all you need. It makes sense, then, to consider the possibility of not really getting it right the first time out, unless you are very lucky.

Starting in a small way will teach you many things, some of which you may have thought of, some of which you couldn't foresee. If you fail you won't have lost a great deal, and you can write it down to experience and start your second project confident of avoiding some of the pitfalls encountered in your first.

This book is designed, of course, to help you increase the chances that your first venture into self-publishing *will* succeed, but no amount of reading can substitute for practical experience of the market and how to deal with it. What this book can do is point you in a suitable direction, and help you look for the most appropriate way forward. Learning business and marketing skills can be a laborious process for photographers whose main aim is simply to be creative with pictures.

In addition to low financial risk, by starting small you can see how the nuts and bolts of marketing, selling and distribution actually work, by doing it yourself. An advantage of doing this is that you have the opportunity to get a feel for the various steps in the chain between taking a picture and seeing the finished image in the shops.

This aspect shouldn't be overlooked. It is all too easy to dismiss what happens after shooting the picture as merely "boring business". Yet I believe that the promotional and financial part of producing a marketable product is probably more important than photographic ability. Once you have a saleable product, this is the make or break work. Those who are ultimately successful have good business heads – or know where to find one!

Thus the self-publisher must be artist, business person, designer, production manager, bill collector, accounts clerk, salesperson, market researcher and distributor. Alternatively, one or some of these activities can be contracted to other people, with a consequent reduction in profit margin. But if you are just beginning, any extra expense is keenly felt.

Let's look at what is involved in these activities in brief; more detailed considerations will be picked up later in the relevant chapters.

Assessing your options

First, of course, you have to consider some of the fundamental aspects of self-publishing: what exactly are you going to publish? And how much time and money can you devote to the project?

In this book I will be emphasising postcards first and foremost, using them as an example of the more general considerations involved. However, each product – postcard, poster, greetings card or whatever – has its own quirks to be thought about, and I will also be discussing these at the appropriate points throughout the book.

In particular, the initial costs of producing a line of postcards pales into insignificance compared with the cost of book production, and distributing postcards in your local area is a far cry from the national distribution of a book.

So an early decision will concern the amount of capital you have, or can borrow. If you borrow money you will have to pay it back according to a schedule.

After finance you need to try and assess the amount of time you have available for this enterprise. Getting round the various outlets with your samples can be a time-consuming affair. If you are launching your product while holding down another job then things could get tough.

Retailers will certainly like to think that you are able to deliver in a reasonable time following an order. Can you do that without compromising other important activities?

Another thing to consider is how you can be contacted by people wishing to buy your goods. If you are a one man or woman band then this could be difficult. An answering machine could be the solution, although not everyone likes talking to a machine. A mobile phone could also meet your requirements; however these are costly and your trade may not justify the expense.

Defining your product

In getting started, however, the most important thing you need is the product. Whatever it is, you should have a well-formed vision of your product and where it will fit into the marketplace.

In the postcard market it will be a hard slog selling a single postcard, however good the image. The market seems not to work like that. What is needed is the right idea for a product line – a collection of postcards.

You may think that the public would be perfectly happy to buy just your card. In fact you may have asked several of them whether they would or not, and the overwhelming response was "yes!". But this is not the point. Your card will be competing for space in a retail outlet.

If the card depicts a local scene then some outlets may take it as it is. These places will most likely be the nearest tourist information centre, or perhaps the local students' union if the card is striking enough and a little bit different. But if your card is a view, however well done, of a local site, then the chances are most straightforward retailers would prefer to see a range of cards covering the area. That way their customers get a choice, your line of cards has more impact, and they get higher volume sales, reducing their relative costs in dealing with your invoice.

Thus your product line will need to fill a market niche. That is, you should consider who will buy the product, at what time of year, and in what quantity. It is a very good idea to have these factors in mind when taking pictures. That way you can gear the type of images you take to the market you hope to compete in.

You will also need to be aware of what else is in your sector of the market. Analyse the competition. This is something many leading producers do. It is virtually indispensable if you hope to succeed.

At the very least your product should match the others on sale. The production values of your cards should be comparable to the competition. They should look as good, feel as good and be perceived to be as good. Otherwise they are likely to fail – unless advertising or other promotional aids give them an edge.

Remember though, it is difficult to sell something that is basically of poor quality. The best way to get a competitive advantage is to produce something a bit different, that people will still buy. You then create a demand that can only be met by your product. This has the considerable plus of your product not selling just on price, but on the intangible extra you have given it. This "intangible" could just be a classy image, which is what you should be good at. Therefore you will not be in fierce competition with bigger rivals who can use mass production to undercut production costs relative to yours.

Design decisions

Once you have got a good image you need to decide on the details of how it will be published.

Say you have thought about the alternatives, and have settled on producing the image as a postcard. Your next step is to consider what kind of postcard. Is the image suitable for a jumbo size or is it better in the conventional size? Should there be a border round the picture, or should the image cover the whole of the card? If a border (or gutter) is chosen, how wide should it be, and should you include a keyline round the image, or put wording on the front?

You might think that postcards all look the same on the back, or reverse, side. Usually the standard is the word "postcard" at the top, a vertical line down the middle dividing the space for the address from the space for writing in, and some words in the lower left hand corner describing the picture and giving the name of the photographer along with a copyright symbol. Even if you don't alter the standard format, you will have to decide what typeface to use for the wording, how big it will be, and of course what it will say.

All the above are design decisions which can dramatically change the "feel" of your product and could make the difference between your postcard being just another on the market, or one which really stands out in the shop. Clearly a sense of design aesthetics helps enormously when dealing with this stage.

As production manager you will need to convey your design decisions to the printers. Clarity of information is essential in this process. Instructions as to layout, production quality, type of finish, size, etc. should be crystal clear. At each point in the production process your job will be to check that you are getting what you want, right down to the final quality control check at the end. It will be your problem if your postcard doesn't sell because its been printed too dark, or you've accepted it with a slight blemish, say a dust spot in the corner.

Promoting yourself

Now you have your product sitting at home waiting to be sold. How are you going to organise this? Mailshot of a brochure, posting samples, personal calling, or what? Are you able to go round likely outlets and talk to the person responsible for buying your type of product?

Photography is often a solitary occupation where the skills that develop are concerned with creative picture taking. Glad-handing may have got left behind in this process, but becomes essential when selling. It may be crucial to your success as a self-publisher when starting out.

It would be desirable to also consider the strategic side of selling, that is, marketing, at this point. Will your postcard become part of a range or line. If so, are you going to introduce the whole line at once, or over several months, or even years? What will your pricing strategy be? Maybe you cannot answer all these questions to start with, but they will have to be thought through at some point, even if the outcome is that you are content with your single image.

What we've considered up to now are factors related to the image and its promotion. Distribution is also important. Basically the product has to be where it will sell – in the outlets. If you are on your own, just beginning, and relatively small scale, then this probably means you will be packaging, invoicing and sending your postcard direct to retailers. You can even do the delivery yourself if your outlets are in a reasonably contained geographical area.

Keeping track

Once you have sold some of your products you will need to get down to the real stuff of business. A delivery note should have accompanied the sale, possibly combined with an invoice. A follow-up statement could be required before payment is forthcoming. Reminders can be necessary for tardy payers.

Business works on trust to a large extent. It is down to your judgement as to who to trust, especially with large orders. On very small scale sales, or where a customer is new to you, you could insist on cash sales only.

The general point is that paperwork needs to be a central part of your business, and that means deciding on your needs and instituting an efficient system to deal with them. Don't forget that you will also have to complete tax returns for the Inland Revenue. The returns will depend on your paperwork. A competent accounting system instituted and run from the start will save an enormous amount of time later, and ensure you claim your full due.

Bear in mind at the outset that your single postcard could turn into a line of cards, these could be joined by other lines to form a product range, and you could diversify into bookmarks, greetings cards and calendars. In other words you could find yourself in full time publishing. Small can grow big.

It is easier to grow big if you get the mechanics of the business running smoothly from the start. Operate efficiently, even if it is on a modest scale. You will understand your finances better, particularly your profit/loss and asset/liability accounts, which will enable you to take informed business decisions rather than shooting in the dark. It is very easy to overlook or discount certain types of costs in the initial stages.

There is a big difference between a hobby which earns a few pounds on the side, and a business the aim of which is to make a worthwhile profit.

Be prepared

At the beginning of a new venture it is easy to overlook the other end – that your product will have a market saturation point. Without experience this point is hard to gauge. Nevertheless it should be borne in mind when starting. It means two things. Be wary about printing too much, or you will be left with unsold stock, and second, start preparing your follow-up products as soon as possible.

Invariably, if your initial sally into the marketplace has been successful, customers will be asking for more. Not more of the same however! More of the similar. The same production values, similar eye-catching images – but definitely something new. It is best therefore to consider your marketing strategy at the outset, or at least have something in mind when selling your first product.

The market is a voracious beast when the product is right. You could find yourself having to make all sorts of excuses for why you are not prepared for the demand. This can sound thoroughly unprofessional and lead to retailers losing confidence in you as a source of supply. Retailers are busy people; they are not too inclined to waste time on those they consider fly-by-nights, or unreliable.

In short, do not sit back and wait to see if your first attempt is going to turn out okay. If you do it will be too late to capitalise on the forward momentum and goodwill you will have built up. Having new images in reserve will not cost you a lot, and will be worth their weight in gold if you have to move quickly with your follow-up.

Your initial and follow-up products should have production values at least as good as those already apparent in other products on the market. It is important to think, not just in terms of your images, but in terms of the overall package you are selling to the customer. The image is the beginning of a process, not the end.

Understanding something of design and production techniques will enable you to make decisions which get you your desired end result. Some knowledge of printing will give you an insight into the range of possibilities available to change the look and feel of your product.

Being conversant with printing terms, and what they mean, also enables you to instruct a printer more fully. Leaving these instructions vague implies to the printer that you are not too concerned about the final appearance of your product and are happy to leave it to them. Fine, if you want to settle for that, but not so good if you know what you really want to achieve.

Marketing and selling

Crucial to the success of your business is the marketing and selling of your product. As a creative image-maker your primary inclination is probably to the taking of photographs. However, persuading the general public to buy them is, in the last analysis, what counts to a self-publisher unless you are concerned only with vanity publishing. You are in business, and the idea of effectively paying someone else to buy your postcards, posters, greetings cards or books should be anathema to you.

Business is about making a profit. Profit is not a dirty word, but represents a means of making more pictures. Obviously you would not be self-publishing if you did not believe in your images, and their worth. The urge to bring them to a wider audience should not be forgotten, but used to motivate your business activity.

Belief in your product is the basis for successful selling. If you have confidence borne of belief you are more than halfway to a sale. If you are not confident, then your customers have no reason to feel like committing themselves to your product.

If your customer is a retailer then you want that person too to be enthusiastic about selling your cards, posters, or books. Put yourself in the position of the public. How often have you been turned off buying because the seller appears not to care?

There is much more to selling of course. A crucial aspect is the price at which you sell, along with the idea that you sell benefits to a purchaser that meet their needs and wants. Thus you need to consider a selling price that reflects your costs, the profit you want, and the perceived value of your product. It is worth giving close attention to these aspects before you commit yourself to making a product.

The product must meet your marketing objectives. In addition you must be able to manufacture your product at a cost which allows you to compete in the marketplace. Thus the cost to you of making, marketing and selling your product must be thought through very carefully.

You don't need to be able to reduce your costs to the level of your rivals, but if you don't, you need to sell at a higher price. To do this means adding value to the product, or increasing its perceived value. Consider whether your images allow you these possibilities.

The artistic route

If some of the foregoing sounds like it will compromise your artistic integrity and does not sit easily with the reasons for your wanting to self-publish, then you should give some serious consideration to alternative ways of bringing your work to the marketplace. Commercial printing and sales methods may not be for you, although you should know what you are missing.

In this case you can explore sales through galleries and craft fairs. Exhibitions, and other forms of self-promotion, can act as your marketing vehicles.

Selling this way entails making products which are "valuable" in themselves. This can be achieved by limiting the number you make, or by using special photographic processes to attain that "fine art" feel.

It is important to realise, however, that to be successful as an artist/self-publisher you still need good business acumen, and at the very least you should possess basic business skills. Selling "art" images still means you are trading and therefore attempting to cover costs at least, if not actually make a profit.

In either event the Inland Revenue will be interested in your activities from the income tax point of view. Thus you will need to make out accounts and so on. Doing this efficiently involves keeping adequate financial records and organising your business properly.

The essential message before you take the plunge, therefore, is to adopt a businesslike attitude from the outset. It will save considerable time and angst later on if you do, whether you print commercially or produce "art" objects for individual sale.

Question your motives

At the end of the day it is essential to ask yourself again: why not get someone else to publish my work?

There is a lot of effort, time, and trouble in publishing yourself. What are your motives for doing so? Is it because you want the satisfaction of seeing your images in print, in exactly the way you want them to appear? Is it the reward of collecting a sizeable portion of the selling price for your work? Is it the sheer pleasure of knowing that you did it all yourself?

Answering yes to these questions means you are well on the way to converting dreams into reality, and entering the excitement and hard work of self-publishing.

CHAPTER CHECKLIST

● Have you thought through what you are trying to achieve with your pictures?

● Have you got a set of images with a theme or thread running through them?

● Have you set your business goals?

● What market do you want to be in?

● Is there a market niche for you?

● What size of self-publishing venture are you interested in?

● Have you got the promotional and financial skills necessary?

● Are you able to be a business person, artist, designer, production manager, bill collector, accounts clerk, salesperson, market researcher and distributor?

● Are you interested in making a profit?

● Have you assessed the amount of time you have available for a self-publishing enterprise?

● Will your images match others on sale?

● Are the production values of your intended product comparable to your competition?

● Is your product idea a bit different to others in the marketplace?

● Have you thought about preparing your follow-up products?

● Do you believe in your ability and your images?

● Are you prepared to to go out and sell your products?

● Have you worked out your likely costs?

● Are you able to produce at a price which allows you to compete?

● What product benefits are you offering to a purchaser that meets their needs and wants?

● Is commercial printing and sales for you?

● Why not get someone else to publish your work?

2 Images

This chapter is concerned with all aspects of the image, but in particular, getting the right image. In the self-publishing context the right image is easy to define – it is the one which both realises your creative input and meets a market need.

However, achieving the ideal balance between artistic intentions and consumer demand is much harder to do than merely talk about. After all, it is possible to create and develop a market demand through producing a product which grabs the popular imagination and sells in bucket-loads. You might think you have such a product.

Stop a moment though, and ask yourself what you are trying to achieve in self-publishing your work. Is it to make lots of money, or is it to bring your vision of things to a wider audience whilst just covering costs? Or is it some midway point between these two extremes?

If your concern is solely as an artist concerned with showing work more widely, then commercial worries can take a back seat. What matters most is whether your artistic intentions will be realised by your self-publishing venture. Provided you have the necessary capital, then other considerations to do with marketing, supply and demand and so on need not interest you when thinking about which type of image to make.

The serious freelance, on the other hand, has to make a living. Thus the primary concern is profitability. Will the venture repay itself and make enough to contribute to daily expenses, at a reasonable rate for the effort involved?

The freelance, therefore, has to think products and markets.

The product line

First you will need to consider what type of product you are going to publish and sell.

One of the first things to ponder is a product line. In other words, a series of images which will constitute the public's perception of what you are selling, and indeed what you are about. It is probably always easier to sell a collection of images which hang together as a coherent group than it is to market a single picture. The exception might be poster reproduction, where strong images stand on their own and there is no expectation among the buying public of seeing a series of related photographs.

In all the other categories discussed in this book – postcards, greetings cards, prints and books – a complete set of images is likely to have the best chance of success. (Of course, a book by definition will need many more than one image; fortunately there is no necessity to bring out more than one book at a time!)

Thus it is sensible to think in terms of a product line, and to concentrate your thoughts on ideas for such a line rather than for just one image.

Consider your customers

So you have in mind a product line, but this is still not enough. The line should ideally fit into a market niche.

Take time out to consider who will buy your product. What type of person are they? What sort of images will appeal to their taste? Which type of retailers stock their type of product? What sort of production values do they like, and what sort of design? Will these factors affect the images you are producing? It is a very good idea to have these thoughts running through your mind when taking pictures. You will then be actively tailoring your photographs to the marketplace. In doing so you will stand a much better chance of filling a need, and hence finding sales, than otherwise.

The foregoing demonstrates the importance of knowing your market and aiming your product at it. This advice is not relevant just to self-publishing ventures of course, but common to almost all freelance activities.

For the same reasons it will pay to analyse the competition. Go to the retail outlets which serve your potential customers and check out the images and products on sale.

Examine their impact, their design element, the way they are presented, their production values, and finally their price. You have to do at least as well visually, for the same cost, in order to make an impression on the buying public.

Bear in mind also that images which make good cards do not necessarily make good posters, and vice versa. The following sections discuss some of the relevant picture considerations for each of the categories being considered in this book. Further marketing issues are raised in a later chapter.

Postcards

Postcards are the category where having a set of cards to offer is more important than in perhaps any other category. It is not just that the public like to see a range of cards to choose from, but retailers are also keen to stock a line.

Some speculation as to why this is so might include the observation that a single card, however interesting, gets "lost" in the postcard rack of a shop. Another is that the reproduced image is small, typically 6x4in, so the impact of a single card is reduced compared to a set where all the individual cards contribute to an overall impression. It might be possible to get round this effect by producing jumbo cards, whose image can be 8x6in, or by publishing a truly arresting image. Even so it is likely a range will do better.

Weaker images may benefit from being part of a set containing very strong images, thus helping to sell them better. Obviously, however, you should try never to include really weak images because the effect could work the other way round. The weak images could drag the whole set down leading to poor or slow sales, which spell marketing death to a range. Remember that the impression which you are trying to create is based on your entire range. If the impression of a creative, impactful set of images remains even with the inclusion of a slightly weak photograph, then you probably have nothing to worry about.

Nonetheless, when doing market research a close watch should be kept on how individual images are received as well as the overall reaction to the range. This happened to me when one of a range of cards I published was printed slightly darker than the rest. The subject matter was not strong enough to combat this effect, and the card was the slowest moving in the outlets. Although initially the range was judged powerful enough to overcome this (by the retailers themselves), the fact that one card was slow-moving began to colour some retailers' perception of the saleability of the cards in general. Luckily this point wasn't reached until sales of the dark image had reached their break-even point, which was handy for me. However, regardless of sales, I clearly needed to withdraw it from the range and replace it with a suitable alternative. Once I had made the switch, reception of the range improved again among those retailers affected.

We'll return to the factors which influence this kind of judgement again from a different angle in the chapter on marketing. Suffice to say here that having to pull images which, for whatever reason, aren't selling, or are selling too slowly, is one reason why most commercial postcard companies pay such low rates for photography. They have to ride

POSTCARD

The Beauty of Manchester
The Opera House
Photography © Nik Chmiel

POSTCARD

Manchester Postcards
Deansgate
Photography © Nik Chmiel

Different printers offer different postcard reverses. Although the reverse is not uppermost in a potential buyer's mind when selecting a postcard, it does add to the overall effect. In the top example, used for the card set pictured on pages 70—71, I wanted a clean-looking and stylish reverse; I opted for type in Palantino Regular and Palantino Italic. In the lower example, used for the set on pages 72—73, I used the more conventional Times Roman type.

the losses. Since you are self-publishing you should endeavour to produce sufficiently strong images so they minimise your losses and maximise your profits.

Postcard themes

In order to produce a range of cards it is fairly obvious that all the cards in the set should follow a similar concept. In short, be thematic!

You might produce cards of local views. If so, try to ensure they all follow a particular idea. For instance, all the images could be photographs of city buildings. Other themes might be the geographical area, building interiors, monuments, people at work in local industry, or more arty themes such as still-lifes or nudes.

Try also to give the range a visual identity in addition to the subject matter. A way of doing this is to take a leaf out of the book of the Gestalt psychologists. They outlined the visual features of the physical world which lead people to group things together. Most relevant here is similarity, of colour or shape say. Thus if all your cards are darkish overall they will tend to be seen as more of a set than if half are brightly coloured. Shape might work if you introduce strong angles into your pictures such that there is an identifiable visual style. In short, each image in the range needs to have a sufficient number of visual elements in common with the other pictures so that they are seen as part of the same set.

Clearly, to give a range an overall feel based on similarity you will need to develop what you want whilst taking the pictures. Trying to do it afterwards will rarely be successful, and a hotchpotch of pictures drawn together in a set will look like just that – a hotchpotch.

You also need to decide what type of postcards you are interested in producing. You could aim for the bottom of the market: straight views of local interest, taken on a bright sunny day – cheap and cheerful, and still very popular. Or you could go for something more moody, creative and artistic. These two products will be for different markets, and likely sold in different retail outlets. Further, they will probably sell in different volumes, and hence be priced differently.

Posters

There are two major differences between posters and postcards which will influence the choice of a suitable image. Firstly, and most obviously a poster image is large. Therefore the image should work as a big picture.

What has impact as a postcard may become overpowering reproduced at 24x20in, or may completely lose its visual point.

One obvious and easy way to determine whether your picture will work as a poster is to get it enlarged to poster size and stick it on the wall. Then check your reaction to it.

The second point about posters is that they frequently contain graphics as well as a picture. These should obviously work together. A clash between a predominantly green image and purple type below is straightforward. But it is possible to destroy that delicate misty landscape with bold type in Times Roman font. The point is that the image and the graphics should reinforce each other in order to promote the effect you want.

Another aspect to consider is that posters need to have general appeal. That is, their subject matter needs to transcend locality or other restricting dimensions. They should be less touristy for example, even if they depict a locality. There are several aesthetic reasons for this which I'll discuss below, but there is also a good marketing reason which arises because posters are difficult to carry – how often do you see sightseers with posters tucked under their arms as opposed to clutching postcards in their hands?

Posters as objects also stand or fall alone. That is, they are one-off purchases, bought for a specific purpose, usually to decorate a room. Their appeal is to a different market niche, therefore, to postcards, because of the end use to which they are put. Your choice of suitable images to become posters needs to reflect this end.

The image must be able to survive on its own, without the reinforcing element that can be present in a range of cards. Just remember when you last bought a poster. You probably had to search through a huge number, one after the other, and all of them very different to each other in style, form, colour and content.

The poster market can be divided roughly into two for present purposes, fine art and gimmicky.

Typically, fine art posters should represent a fantasy mood or offer something beyond mere record. Generally posters in this category are not aimed at informing; they are not directed at conveying information such as what a particular location looks like. In contrast to postcards this type of product should be perceived as art, and their appeal should rest to some extent on the feeling or emotion they induce when looking at them. Hence your choice of image should reflect this. Romance or escapism are often good sellers for example. The aesthetic quality should be evident and there is a lot of skill in producing images of a high enough standard.

"Gimmicky" posters do not necessarily place such a great demand on aesthetic qualities because the impact of the poster, and the reason it is bought, is based on the gimmick itself, and this often depends on a word-picture combination. Their appeal can range from humour, through irony, to pathos.

Posters also need to be able to stand being hung on a wall for a considerable length of time, depending on the type of poster. The more gimmicky ones might last a few months until the novelty wears off, but fine art posters can remain up for years.

Greetings cards

Greetings cards serve very specific purposes; they convey a message. For example: "Thinking of You", "I Love You", "Happy Birthday", "Merry Christmas", "Be my Valentine".

Clearly the image has to be illustrative of the message, or connected to it in some way, often by popular association. Thus some types of greeting card image are tightly constrained.

A Valentine card very frequently has a red rose on it, whether it is a sexy card or a gushingly romantic one. Birthday cards often feature balloons and streamers, and so on. Of course your cards do not have to follow the trend – after all if they were slavish copies of what is already in the market they probably wouldn't sell.

The point is, however, that in this sector of the market you need to be very aware of the visual conventions that exist. They are there for a reason: they help sell cards.

Books

Finally we turn to books. In some senses self-publishing books is a very different enterprise to the card and poster categories we have discussed so far. They require a much greater capital outlay for example. But in the terms of this chapter, they place very different requirements on image selection. Quintessentially books are about a body of images which should work together.

I mentioned a type of coherence in imagery when I discussed postcard ranges. There are several differences however. Immediately apparent is that you need only buy one postcard from a range, whereas when you buy a book you buy all the images in it – those you like and those you may not. Second, there are many more images in a book, typically 50-plus, whereas a postcard range may comprise between 8 and 24 images at any one time. Third, it would be surprising to find all the images in a book adhering to the basic grouping principles I outlined earlier.

Nonetheless the images in a book should work together, and appear of a piece. This means that the dimensions along which the pictures work will likely be far more subtle than the purely visual ones I have talked about in connection with postcards, involving greater aesthetic consideration on your part, and on that of the buyer.

Again, look at the market. Most books have a discernible style to them, although it may not be obvious at first. I'll return to what this style is and what the possible dimensions are in a moment, but first I want to consider a further important aspect of images in books. This is that they form a sequence.

This is an important point to grasp. The images you choose to include in your book should work, not just together, but as a sequence of images. Such a sequence can be capable of conveying considerably more than any one of the constituent images, or indeed the same collection of images sequenced unsympathetically. Study one of Ralph Gibson's books to see what I mean. He formed a publishing company in order to realise his images in print. Self-publishing certainly worked for him!

It is also easy to tell a book is by Ralph Gibson just by looking at the images. He has a clear, discernible, minimalist approach, different to most other photographers. For the type of book he is interested in publishing, and for the type of things he wishes to say photographically, his approach is that of the artist choosing both his medium and means of expression.

Not all photographic books need fall into this category. An opposite extreme would be a book illustrating a geographical area. The demand here would be for pictorial representation.

However, it is worth considering your reactions when you see a book of photographs. Do you notice a consistent approach to the book's content, and do you prefer consistency to otherwise? I find my preference is very much towards consistency, and feel that it helps create the impression of a unified vision. So much so in fact, that images which fall outside the dominant style and approach really jar. This certainly affects my buying decisions. This is not to argue that all pictures in a book should look identical – far from it! My point is that they should fit a discernible approach to subject matter.

A third category of books which you may be interested in producing is that of "how to" books. Here your pictures will be used as illustration, to support points made in the text. Image choice should reflect this, rather than aesthetic consideration. The main criterion is that the images should convey information. Nonetheless they should be technically excellent, and also visually coherent. So, while not the main focus of a "how to" book, the way the images hang together as a series should still be in the back of your mind when choosing what to include and what to leave out.

In general, it is a good idea to produce a book dummy when contemplating self-publishing your images in book form. A dummy is a mock up of the book with all the images in sequence, and preferably to the size they will appear when printed. To save on costs, and to retain flexibility while you are still sorting out the sequencing, you could make photocopies of your prints and put them into a ring binder or something similar. Then you can play around with the order of the images without damaging expensive prints.

Once you are satisfied with the way you have run the pictures you can introduce any text needed. When you are happy with your result you can produce a second dummy with photographic prints instead of photocopies.

This dummy can then serve for your market research. You will want to gather reactions to your book project and determine whether it is financially viable. This is a step which should also be taken for any other self-publishing venture you are engaged in, be it postcards, posters or whatever. Read the chapter on marketing before launching into production.

I have discussed some of the points concerning image selection from an aesthetic point of view. Next I want to discuss technical considerations which help to produce those images.

Equipment and quality

The right equipment for you is the camera, lenses and accessories which enable you to produce the kind of image you want. This is very easy to say, of course, but also very true.

The right equipment is not about this manufacturer or that, or about expensive versus cheap lenses, or about autofocus versus manual lenses and cameras. If it is your intention to produce blurred, grainy photographs, then hand-holding a cheap lens on an old camera will probably do the trick. If on the other hand you are after bitingly sharp images when enlarged to A2 poster size, then a large or medium format camera, slow film and a heavy tripod are pretty well essential.

This section, then, will discuss some of the general aspects of equipment needed to achieve particular end results, rather than concentrating on individual pieces of gear. Nonetheless, I will be mentioning what I use, and why, to give some reference points for your own thoughts.

The discussion will centre on those characteristics of film, format, cameras, lenses and accessories which contribute to producing an image ready for reproduction. In particular I will consider the photographic aspects which can be abstracted from any image, independent of content. First, quality – as represented by resolution, contrast, colour saturation and tonal gradation; and second, sharpness, encompassing depth of field and the plane of focus.

Film format: Starting with film formats is the most logical place to begin a discussion of quality because, all other things being equal, the choice of format bears more directly on the end image than many of the more mechanical aspects of equipment.

The choice of format influences two things directly, assuming no cropping – image shape, and image quality; and one other thing indirectly – method of working.

There are three format classes: small, medium and large. Film in the small format includes 110, half-frame and 35mm sizes, with 35mm being the pre-eminent choice. This is for good reason. There is a huge variety of film speeds and makes to choose from, giving an enormous control over the end result. In addition, 35mm is almost certainly the minimum acceptable size for adequate reproduction of published images, unless very low quality results are part of your artistic intentions. This is not just a question of grain or blur, it is also that colour saturation and tonal gradations suffer when small film sizes are enlarged to required levels. For these reasons I will only talk about 35mm here as representative of the small format. Its actual size is 24x36mm.

Medium format sizes range from 6x4.5cm, 6x6cm, 6x7cm to 6x9cm. This represents a considerable choice of image shape. Large format sizes include 5x4in, 7x5in, 10x8in and 11x14in – the most common being 5x4in, followed by 10x8in.

Medium and large format negatives produce a significant increase in quality over 35mm for the same size enlargement. The gain is not just in resolution in the finished result, but also in colour saturation and tonal subtlety. It is easy to see the reason for this. If a frame-filling image is produced on the same emulsion on 35mm, 6x4.5cm, 6x6cm, 6x7cm, 6x9cm, 5x4in, and 10x8in sizes, then the number of silver grains that can be involved in reproducing that image on the negative or transparency will be in the approximate ratio 1 : 3 : 4 : 5 : 6 : 14 : 58. You can appreciate therefore, that with the larger formats, more image forming emulsion is utilised for each part of the image, leading to better resolution, saturation, and reproduction of tonal variations.

To put this another way, if the aim is to enlarge each image to a standard 10x8 inch print, then certain film sizes need to be cropped, and the area magnification of each negative or transparency would be about x69.5, x20, x17.5, x13.5, x11, x4, x1 respectively. Area, not linear, magnification is the correct measure because when an enlargement is made the image is expanded in two dimensions. Thus the same number of information-carrying silver grains in the original image are spread out in both vertical and horizontal directions.

Only you will be able to judge whether you need to use larger image sizes to get what you want in terms of quality factors, bearing in mind the size and shape of the finished, reproduced product.

As an attempt to get a handle on what is needed lets consider the magnifications required for the standard postcard size (6x4 inches) and an A2 poster (24x16 inches). For the postcard the area magnifications for each of the different format sizes are x17.5, x6.5, x6.5, x4.5, x3, x1.5, x0.5 approximately. For the A2 poster the magnifications would be x278, x100, x100, x74.5, x44.5, x23.5, x6 respectively.

The comparison of these magnifications with those for enlarging to a standard 10x8in print are very interesting. This is because most people find 10x8in enlargements from 35mm very acceptable in quality terms, and whilst seeing the difference between a 35mm and 6x7cm enlargement at this size, would not consider it that important, at least in terms of resolution if not tonality.

So for example, if you were producing postcards where high quality was required, then the magnification from 35mm would be 17.5, far less than that needed for a 10x8in print. 17.5 is the enlargement necessary from a 6x6cm negative to produce a 10x8in print. Therefore, all other things being equal, 35mm will produce the same quality on a postcard as 6x6cm would on a 10x8in print.

Of course all things are usually not equal when considering this comparison. However, the other factors may actually increase your bias to choose 35mm for postcard production. For instance, the top makers' 35mm lenses are often the best you can get, thus at negative level the resolution on film may be better than other formats. Also, one of the finest films, Kodachrome 25, is only available in 35mm size.

The situation alters completely when the A2 poster is considered. Here, to get the same quality as 35mm would give on a 10x8in print it would be necessary to use a negative size of 6x7cm. The message, therefore, is that it is always sensible to consider the end product when deciding on film formats in relation to quality.

Aspects other than size also count towards the assessment of quality and I will turn to these next. These are film speed, lens quality and taking conditions.

Film speed & type: The general rule with film speed is that the slower the film, the better the ability of the film to resolve fine detail, and hence the better the quality. In colour, film speeds much above ISO 100 will start to look grainy compared to their slower counterparts. In black and white the equivalent speed is probably ISO 400.

Within each speed bracket different films have differing resolution abilities and differing image qualities and contrast. For example, the two best slide films currently on the market, in my experience, are Fuji Velvia and Kodachrome 25. In terms of resolution these films barely differ, but Velvia is contrasty and reproduces colours very brightly and with high saturation – great for a dull day or where the lighting is very even. Kodachrome 25, on the other hand, handles contrasty lighting very well, and reproduces reds and yellows in a vibrant, attractive way. It is good in bright, sunny light outdoors.

However that is not the end of it. Fuji Velvia can be push and pull processed at least by one stop without appreciable loss in resolving ability. This allows considerable control over the final contrast in the image.

An example using black and white films illustrates further fine distinctions between films. Kodak T-Max 400 is a fine film, capable of good resolution. Its main characteristic however, is a lovely creamy texture to the images it produces. This can be contrasted with Kodak Tri-X, another ISO 400 film. This too is capable of good reproduction, but produces quite a different feel, much harder or colder in tone. Clearly there is no substitute for experimentation when it comes to choosing the film or films that will serve your particular purposes.

Before leaving the topic of film speed and type, it is important to consider the reproduction needs of the published end-product you are aiming for. Many printing houses are set up for reproducing colour, and reproduction from transparencies – that is from reversal film – is often better in quality terms, size for size. Some printers even reproduce black and white using the four-colour process. This will be discussed further in the chapter on production techniques.

Obviously some compensation can enter decisions about film type since a print from a large format colour negative will reproduce very well. Examples in books by Joel Meyorwitz and others demonstrate this.

Lens quality: Lens quality in relation to the production of an image is a function primarily of resolution, contrast, and accuracy, by which I mean the faithful reproduction of the shapes of objects. This assumes that basic aberrations have been designed out or minimised, which tends to be the case with modern computer-aided design procedures. There are additional factors, such as freedom from flare, even illumination across the frame, and consistency at all apertures and focusing distances, which I think are important too, particularly to the utility of a lens under a variety of conditions.

Perceived sharpness in an image appears to be the function of resolution and contrast. Very high resolution lenses still appear less sharp if they are of low contrast than less good lenses of higher contrast. These factors are difficult to gauge from published tests, which tend to concentrate only on resolution. If possible you should try lenses before you buy to check they give you the result you want.

High quality is only necessary if you want sharp, contrasty pictures. If, for example, you are trying to recreate a postcard series with an old-fashioned pre-war look, you might well hunt down old, uncoated, flary lenses.

As already mentioned above, 35mm lenses from top makers are extremely good, and probably out-resolve other formats. This is because they are easier to manufacture to the necessary standard. But even at this level professional lenses do not come cheaply. Leitz lenses, for example, which are easily among the best you can buy for 35mm cameras, cost as much, and sometimes more, than medium or large format equivalents.

Cameras: In relation to quality, the job of a camera is to hold the film flat, to allow the correct amount of light in through the shutter, and to keep out any extraneous, non image-forming light. Almost all modern cameras succeed in these respects.

Of course they differ considerably in other matters such as the exposure modes on offer, and features such as self-timers etc. Choices about these are very personal. Ease of use and being comfortable with your cameras is probably more important in the long run than the latest gizmo.

The other main quality consideration is that the camera works consistently, time and time again, in different conditions from the heat of the studio to the cold of a winter morning outdoors.

Meters: You may wonder what exposure meters have to do with quality. In the main it is to do with consistency of the final image for publication. As was discussed earlier with regard to coherence in a range of postcards, it is important to be able to produce images which look the same with regard to overall brightness. Bright images look different to darker ones, and may be treated as different by retailers and the buying public, leading to a judgement that your range does not hang together. Therefore your metering technique needs to be such as to enable you to produce transparencies and prints of consistent density.

In my experience of producing images of outdoor scenes and buildings, the best technique is to use an incident lightmeter. This measures the light falling on a scene, rather than the light reflected from it. The great advantage of this technique is that tonal variations in the subject do not influence the exposure reading. This leads to very consistent settings, where each subject tone is referenced to the incident reading. For example a dark brown, stone-faced building will reproduce as such, and a bright white wall will be rendered faithfully.

The key here is that the tones will always reproduce referenced to the incident reading (which is equivalent to 18% reflectance). So if you feel that you are consistently underexposing your photographs, because all tones are reproduced too dark, it is easy to adjust your reference by a fixed amount, yet still maintain consistency.

This is not possible with reflectance meters with a wide acceptance angle, which give readings that are a function of the tonal values in a scene, and thus change with subject matter. The exception is a spot-meter which has a very narrow angle of acceptance. The best measure a 1 degree spot. This enables the photographer to precisely measure the reflectance from a single tone, and thus make an exposure which will place this tone anywhere he or she chooses on the film's sensitivity profile. This technique requires considerably more experience to produce consistent results, needing a firm understanding of subject tonal values. It does, however, allow great precision, although it is time consuming to use, in contrast to the incident technique.

Another advantage of the latter arises when you are using transparency film which is very demanding of accurate exposure – you can be sure that bright highlights will never burn out on film.

If you have no experience of incident and spot metering and so do not appreciate what I have just written, then I urge you to consult a book specifically concerned with these exposure methods. It is well worth while. The use of an incident technique will require the use of a separate hand-held exposure meter, no bad thing in my opinion, even if your camera has a built-in meter.

Tripods: Tripods help produce high quality results. There is no way round this fact. Even at high shutter speeds hand-held results can often be improved by using a sturdy tripod. For slow speeds they are all but essential. For large, and most medium format, cameras they are a necessity.

This does not mean to say you need always use a tripod, merely that there is a quality trade-off if you do not. The trade-off may well be acceptable to you, and more pertinently, to your customers.

If you do decide you need a tripod for your image-making, then ensure it is big enough, and heavy enough, and firm enough, to cope with your camera and lenses. A flimsy, wobbly, tripod is worse than having none at all. I have found those made by Linhof and Manfrotto to be very good.

Filters: Filters are an extra piece of glass or plastic placed between film and subject, and therefore form one more element which can diffract and diffuse image forming light. Thus there is a quality cost to using filters, which can be minimised by buying good quality ones which do not scratch easily.

Again good quality is not cheap, but there are some surprisingly good filters which are not too expensive. One such range is the Cokin P series, although it lacks a true neutral density graduated filter. It has instead a graduated grey, which of course introduces a grey cast as well as reducing the transmission of light in the appropriate part of the filter. It is possible to have other filter makers make up a true ND graduate in the Cokin size.

Bags: Why should bags be mentioned in a section on quality? Well, mainly because a good bag helps keeps equipment clean and away from the elements. Clean lenses especially are important to producing sharp, contrasty images.

I use soft bags when shooting outdoors, and have found the Domke range to be excellent. For carrying equipment, especially when it is heavy, over long distances I use a LowePro Phototrekker. This is a backpack which has movable dividers that allow almost any shape camera to be accommodated. I carry a metal 5x4 inch view camera, two lenses and accessories in it with no problem.

Sharpness: I have singled out sharpness, as represented by the plane of focus and depth of field, from the other aspects of quality mentioned above, because it is under the photographer's control every time a picture is taken. These aspects therefore need to be considered each time an image is produced.

In general I think the buying public expect images to be sharp from front to back when looking at a photograph, unless there is a clear intention on the part of the photographer to use differential focus or blur for artistic reasons. I don't know why this expectation appears to exist, although I would speculate that our visual prejudices are governed to some extent by painters and the fact that our visual systems accommodate sufficiently quickly to objects near and far. Paintings almost never have out of focus effects in them. They may use atmospheric haze to denote distant parts of a scene, but that is different.

Plane of focus: The plane of focus is just that plane in a scene where everything on the plane is brought into sharp focus on the film. That is, a point of light on the plane is reproduced as a point of light on the film. Any point not on the plane is not reproduced as a point on the film, but as a circle of some diameter which increases the further the point is from the plane.

In cameras where the lens is fixed in relation to the film – that is for most small and medium format cameras – the plane is perpendicular to the lens axis, and its distance from the camera is determined by the focusing of the lens.

In some medium format cameras, and almost all large format cameras, it is possible to move the lens independently of the film. This means that the plane of focus need not be perpendicular to the lens axis, and can be made to lie at an angle, its relationship to the film being governed by the Scheimpflug principle. Using this principle allows objects near to the camera, and those far away, to be on the same plane of focus, and hence be maximally sharp.

Why should focus be so important?

The main reason is that the subject you wish to represent in your image should be in focus, that is as sharp as possible. Visual convention and taste dictate it. Without it your image is very unlikely to sell. That means focusing is critical to your images. It therefore pays dividends to use any focusing aid which helps get critical focus.

All cameras which use a ground glass screen to focus on – and that means all 35mm SLRs, all medium format SLRs and TLRs, and all large format view and monorail cameras – need a bright focusing screen. Fresnel lenses help here, and it is possible to buy special bright screens from Beattie and others. Modern 35mm SLRs tend to be very good in this respect and are generally ahead of other formats.

The alternative is to use range-finder focusing, or auto-focus cameras. Range-finder cameras bring two overlapping images into register when focus is correct. It is usually easy to tell when this happens, and with wide to normal angle lenses focusing is more accurate than with SLRs. However their advantage is lost with lenses longer than 135mm on the 35mm format.

Auto-focus cameras use a passive infrared system to ensure accurate focus, and are a boon if your eyesight is less than perfect.

Once critical focus is established the next aspect of sharpness to consider is depth of field.

Depth of field: Depth of field refers to the distance in front of and behind the plane of focus which is acceptably sharp to the viewer.

As mentioned above most people expect photographs to be sharp from front to back. What this really means is that the main subject should be in sharp focus, while less important areas can be acceptably sharp. Thus distant background can be out of focus to a degree, as can very near foreground, but only if it is not crucial to the composition.

It is worth noting that for any given angle of view, medium and large format lenses have less depth of field. However this does not automatically make 35mm better, because shape-defining properties, such as colour saturation, mean that out of focus elements can often appear more substantial with the medium or large format lenses, for any particular size of enlargement.

So whatever the technical properties of format, lens and enlargement, the key arbiter is subjective. It is what looks right, and is acceptable to those buying the image, which counts.

I have found that for postcard-sized reproduction 35mm equipment of good quality produces saleable images which look sharp and have good colour saturation. If I wanted the same standard of sharpness and colour saturation in a poster, however, I would look to medium or large format cameras and film.

Processing: After all the effort made to choose the right equipment and film for your purposes it would be downright perverse to be sloppy with processing. The greatest pictures can be ruined by cheap run-of-the-mill processing. If you are intent on producing publishable images it is essential to find a good processing laboratory, and then to stick with them. The lab you settle on should ideally offer all the processing services you need, plus those you might need in the future.

The standard you should look for is perfection. Transparencies should be perfectly reproduced and free of scratch and drying marks. If you ask for them mounted they should be cut perfectly, mounted flat, and with no glue or fingerprints on them. Prints should be reproduced exactly to your specification. Do not accept excuses, it is your money and reputation that is on the line if processing is sub-standard.

Clearly perfection is not cheap, therefore expect to pay a reasonable price for it. Some labs charge for push and pull processing, some do not.

More subtly, different labs may process the same film stock in slightly different ways. For example my usual lab seems to get an extra degree of luminosity into my Fujichrome slides compared to another lab I've used regularly in the past, even though the processing standards at both labs are roughly equivalent.

Editing

It is now time to talk about one of the most important aspects of getting the right image – editing.

The value of good editing should not be underestimated. It is crucial, of course, in selecting from a range of photographs you have already taken, but the editing decisions you make then will also be in your mind the next time you are using your camera. Thus a professional approach to editing will not only lead to your best images being chosen for your publication project, it will also help to sharpen your "eye" for a good picture next time around.

The process of editing should be split into two stages: technical and aesthetic. The technical stage is concerned solely with the quality of the image. The aesthetic stage is where your subjective reactions come into the process in order to let you determine whether your photographic intentions have been achieved. So let's start with the technical phase.

The technical stage should be a quite mechanical process of weeding out all those pictures which are out-of-focus, badly exposed – that is highly over or under-exposed – and blurred.

During this process it is important to be as detached as possible from the picture content. Okay, that picture is a one-off shot impossible to repeat, that one is the only one where the light was magic, and so on, but try to ignore these little nagging thoughts. If the picture is technically flawed, throw it out. It won't do.

Your self-published work should be as professional as possible in the technical sense. The discerning public who are hopefully going to buy your images will expect photographic competence. They are unlikely to buy poor quality images, and worse, they may well end up associating your name with low quality and therefore not buy anything else you produce either.

So the message is: be ruthless. Your task is to at least match the quality levels already on the market. It will therefore pay to study what is already on the market in your chosen field. Remember that quality may also be associated with price point, so check for this, but it is unlikely that any product will be below a certain threshold of quality.

Editing for the market

Once the pictures showing poor technical merit have been weeded out you can turn to picking the images which will be part of your final product. The dimensions which should form at least a part of this stage in the editing process are composition, "feel", density and colour. The aim is to choose images with impact, and which form part of a range where appropriate.

Your images have to communicate: a sense of place, a feeling, a desire and so on. The buying public has to like your images enough to part with hard-earned money. They need to feel they are getting something for their money, a product with which they are happy. Any old snapshot will not do. Your images must have allure, and now is the time to select those that do.

Bear in mind that although the images you chose now may satisfy you, they may not meet the desires of a wider audience. Thus you may want to do a little market research using friends and relations who you can trust to be critical and honest. You are not after praise unless it is genuine. Whether you turn to other opinions to help make your judgement is a personal matter, and will depend largely on whether you feel you yourself represent, or are typical of, the market you are trying to sell into. This is hard to gauge initially.

Of course if your aim is simply to bring your art to the public, then artistic considerations should be uppermost. Does the chosen image represent what you intended to say visually?

Once the editing process is over you will have an image, or a range which hangs together, which you will be ready to feed into the production process.

CHAPTER CHECKLIST

● Have you chosen the images which both realise your creative input and meet a market need?
● Have you thought about products and markets?
● Do your images hang together as a coherent group?
● Have you actively tailored your photographs to the marketplace?
● Did you analyse the competition?
● Do the images chosen for your products match the impact, the design elements, the presentation and the production values of others in the marketplace?
● Can you produce uniformly strong images for your range?
● Are any of the images likely to drag the whole set down, leading to poor or slow sales?
● Does your range of cards follow a similar concept?
● Do your poster images have general appeal?
● Do your poster images work as a big picture?
● Do your greetings card images convey a message?
● Have you got enough images which form a coherent sequence to form a book?
● Have you got the right equipment to produce the kind of image you want?
● Have you used the appropriate film format, film speed & film type?
● Does your lens have your desired combination of resolution, contrast and accuracy?
● Do your pictures have the appropriate degree of sharpness, as represented by the plane of focus and depth of field?
● Have you found a good processing laboratory?
● Have you edited your images for technical excellence?
● Have you edited your images for composition, "feel", density and colour?
● Does each chosen image represent what you intended to say visually?

3 Production

This chapter is about the process of turning the image you have into an end product, either a postcard, poster, greetings card or book. Topics covered include the product and production values, costing considerations, and the design and manufacture of the product.

Although all these factors are distinct parts of the production process they also interact. It will therefore benefit you to read through the whole of this chapter. If you choose to select only bits of it, it will be more difficult to understand the whole process.

The product

One of the first things to think about at the beginning of the production process is what it is you want to produce. This may sound a bit like putting the cart before the horse; however it is difficult to make a product unless you can visualise the final outcome – that is, exactly what it is you want to achieve.

The image which you have laboured hard to find is only the beginning of the production process, even though at this stage you may be feeling that you've got a great image or set of images and the rest should be easy.

No way; your image has to be reproduced, and this stage is every bit as important as getting that amazing image in the first place. It is quite possible to ruin the impact, and hence sales, of even the best image with poor design and reproduction.

Thus the next step after you've selected your images is to consider how they will appear as a product in the marketplace. Anything which can aid this process of visualisation will be helpful.

One means is to spend time in your favourite card, poster and book shops. What you're looking for is what is selling: the visual style.

Clearly you do not want simply to copy what you find there; if you did you would just be entering an already crowded arena. However, the question in your mind should be centred round the look you are going to give to your product, whether it will sell if it is very different to the other products on sale, how it will fit into the market environment, and what will it look like on the shelves next to the competition.

Costing

The second important aspect to have in mind when checking out the competition is what price products like the ones you intend to market are selling for. In order to compete you will have to bring in the same quality at the same price. This will dictate how much you can spend on designing and printing, which in turn will affect the look and feel of your product.

This point is probably more important in the poster and card markets than in books, where diversity is expected. Nonetheless, perceived value will still be important to some extent, even in the latter market. If this sounds like being too commercial then so be it. If your concern is to make an artistic impact on the world you will still need to finance your vision.

It is useful at this stage to get quotes on costs from printers. The printer you choose to carry out your printing job is very important. Different printers are better at some things than others, and some are specialists. It depends on your product as to which one you choose.

Commercial printers which specialise in business printing such as brochures, company cards, flyers, etc. should be able to print postcards and greetings cards, and some may do posters. Printers able to produce books and those capable of producing fine art posters are more specialised, and therefore may be more expensive for the simpler products like postcards. Shop around to find a suitable printer at a suitable price.

Many printers will send you sample packs of the type of printing service they offer. Study these carefully. The printer should be sending you what that company considers to be their best product. It is their advertisement for their wares. Ask yourself whether the samples meet your quality level and whether the price is right. I will pick up the quality/price printing equation in the section on manufacture later in the chapter.

Most prices will be related to the quantity that you order. The price per postcard is much cheaper if you have 5,000 printed in one run than if you print 1,000, followed by another thousand and so on. However this does not mean you should simply print the largest number you can afford. Bear in mind that your product will have a market saturation point – shopkeepers will get bored with it even if customers are still buying. The point is not to print too much.

How much to go for in the beginning is a question of the market size and location, the likely popularity of your product, and the effort you can put into marketing and selling it. These things are very difficult to judge without experience. Ask as many people as you can about the volume of business they do in your market sector. Retailers have no need to treat such information as commercially sensitive, although other producers might.

The basic approach being taken in this chapter is that existing products in the marketplace will determine the ball-park figure you can charge for your products, and hence the amount of money you have available to spend on production. However, the price you set for your product must also cover marketing, selling and distribution costs. All these need to be taken into account when pricing, and when deciding what you can afford for actual production.

Finance

It is obvious that any self-publishing activity will need adequate financing. The best way to do this is to have your own money. Self-funding your own publishing will mean no interest repayments and debt schedules. Hence you will avoid some of the problems, such as cash flow due to loan pay back dates, due to borrowing cash.

Other sources of capital are bank loans, or borrowing from family and friends.

If you are borrowing from a bank you will need a business plan. This should include outgoings and a projection of income over a period, often a year or more. The business plan needs to be well thought out, otherwise it will not be convincing, and worse, may lead you into false hopes. If you base your spending on erroneous projections in your business plan you could end up in debt with sorry consequences. You will also need to convince the bank that you have a viable product and have thought about the market your product will sell in.

Make sure you get good advice on the financial aspects involved in borrowing money to float your self-publishing venture. Try to project expenses for a three year period, and calculate your possible income given various contingencies. Be hard-nosed rather than over-optimistic. These aspects are dealt with in much greater detail in the chapter on business matters.

It may well pay you to think small at first. You will gain experience, and with it confidence in your own judgement without risking too much. Make sure you build in realistic margins of profitability. It is too easy to shave your profit in order to float a venture and then find you have a shortage of capital to take you on to the next project or to capitalise on initial success. Give value for money, but don't sell yourself short.

Design

Design is at the heart of the production process. The final look of your product which the buyer will see in the shops depends on the visual style and feel created by the design of the overall package. The image or images and their context should harmonise to produce an appealing product which the public will purchase. For this reason you should certainly make sure that adequate finance is available for good design if you are not able to do it yourself.

Before discussing individual markets I will consider some general principles.

A key aspect is to create a uniform look for your product line. This is very important as even strong images can look distinctly odd if they do not carry the general look and feel of other pictures with which they will be compared in your range or book.

It will pay therefore, to be thematic in your approach. For example if you are going to publish a postcard range, concentrate on a particular geographic area, or a singular approach such as photographing every picture in a misty way, or try to stick to one concept, such as all buildings or all people.

Design is very important but it should not overwhelm your postcard or poster. For example, if your poster is of a delicate pastel hue then heavy black lettering will destroy the light feel of the picture. However, keep in mind the end use of the product. If it is a poster it may well be framed, and therefore this too should be designed in. If you do this frame shops should like it, and home framers will also appreciate not losing the impact of the image.

Product testing

Once you have finished a pleasing design, create a mock-up of it. Try to get the mock-up as close as possible to how you envision the final appearance of the product. Do not skimp on this process, because when you ask for reactions to your mock-up you want the responses to be as close as possible to those you will get to the product itself.

Next you can take the mock-up to retailers in your area to test their reactions and see whether they would stock products based on the mock-up. Take some time to think of all the possible outlets, and try to elicit as full a set of comments as possible: do they like it; will they buy it; what quantities will they take; at what time of year? If you can, do the same for distributors.

Testing your product on retailers and distributors is a much more stringent test than getting your friends to say whether they would buy your goods. Retailers and distributors are in business and need to make money through what they handle and sell. They should therefore have a far better idea of the market than your friends. Of course the latter are important in the initial stages of taking and editing images and in getting emotional support for your venture. At this later stage, however, you want hard-headed advice with no punches pulled. After all, if you get it wrong now it is your money which will be lost.

Market research and how to do it is covered in greater depth in the chapter on marketing.

Manufacture

The remainder of this chapter is concerned with the physical manufacture of your product. By and large this will concern the printing of visual images. However, posters can involve text and image combinations, while postcards require text on the reverse and sometimes on the front as well. Books naturally concern the merging of image and text.

I will focus on image manufacture first and foremost, and mention text styles and reproduction where appropriate.

The place to start when trying to appreciate the production process is with printing – the nuts and bolts of getting a photographic image on to paper.

Part of the visualisation of your product depends on knowing what happens at the printing stage and considering the variables that can affect it. It is sensible to try to understand at least some of the printing process as you will need to instruct a printer when you come to make your images into a final product. Being able to speak a few words in the printer's language helps.

It is quite possible to specify exactly what you want in terms of the finished image. It should therefore be up to the printer to give you what you want. Unfortunately, like any manufacturing process, there are limitations to what a printer can do for you. Knowing about these and why they arise will avoid disappointment, expense and argument at a later stage.

Printing processes

It is possible to obtain very fine quality reproduction using modern printing presses. There are three main methods of commercial reproduction: letterpress, lithography and gravure.

Letterpress is like a typewriter in that it uses a raised surface to print from. Parts of the image which are to be reproduced lighter are etched or gouged out of the surface, which is then inked. The surface is then pressed on to the paper to transfer the image.

Lithography works by treating a thin metal sheet so that the areas to print dark will not retain moisture. The sheet is then wetted, and inked. The ink only holds in the non-wet (i.e. dark) areas because it is grease-based and the ink and moisture do not mix. Commercial lithography processes use the offset principle, whereby the litho sheet is contacted with a rubber blanket, transferring the image to it. The blanket is then brought into contact with the paper, hence the "offset". This process is now very widespread, and is likely to be the process you will use.

Gravure is the reverse of letterpress. The parts of the image to print dark are etched into the metal, and then filled with ink. The metal is then wiped clean and brought into contact with the paper, which absorbs ink from the hollows in the metal.

There are advantages and disadvantages to all three means of printing. Letterpress allows the use of dense inks and gives good printing of type for high quality books. However it is a relatively slow process which requires more expensive paper to get the same quality as other processes. The preparation of the printing surface is expensive.

Offset litho gives good reproduction of detail and photographs, and is relatively cheap to prepare. The use of the offset rubber blanket enables the use of a wider range of papers and the printing is relatively quick. It is harder, however, to produce a dense ink film, and colour variations can arise because the ink/water balance can change over a long print run.

Gravure allows a more consistent colour to be maintained during printing and gives good results on cheaper and lighter paper. However the plates are expensive to produce and the process is only viable for very long print runs. It is mainly used for newspapers and colour supplements.

Origination

All these printing processes need some type of "origination" from the image, which is then used as the basis for etching or treating the metal from which the print will be made.

For the letterpress and lithographic methods the printing is all or none. Either the surface has ink which contacts the paper (for the dark areas) or not (for the light areas). With these methods what is needed is a means of producing shades of grey between black and white. These shades of grey must reflect the tones in the original image.

The basis for this origination is the halftone dot. Tones are converted into a fine pattern of dots of different sizes. Thus printed black and white photographs are really made up of a mosaic of black dots and clear spaces. The ratio of dots to spaces determines the shade of grey the eye perceives. This is because at normal viewing distance the dots and spaces, if sufficiently dense (about 5 – 6 per mm), merge into a tone due to limitations in the eye's resolving ability.

The image is turned into a halftone pattern by copying it through a soft-edged screen or ruled grid. If the screen ruling is fine more dots are produced from the image, which allows more detail to be shown. However, the fineness of the screen ruling you can use is limited by the type of paper to be used for printing. If the paper is very absorbent the dots will merge into one another, producing a smudgy effect because the tones then run into one another.

Gravure also uses a screen to produce halftones, but the effect is different. More ink is deposited in the dark areas than in the lighter ones, and hence transferred to the paper. Thus the changes in density on the printed reproduction are due to ink density rather than an optical trick as in lithography.

Origination methods

Screened originations are created using a process camera, or a scanner. With the advent of colour printing and the common use of offset lithography, most modern images are scanned, even those for black and white reproduction.

A process camera is a large version of an ordinary camera, and screened images are made by exposing film in a similar way to taking a picture, but interposing a screen between the lens and film. When black and white reproduction is requested the screen is often oriented at an angle of 45 degrees to the horizontal in order to make the rows of dots less obvious to the eye. Image size can be altered at this stage. The end result is either a screened negative or screened positive which can be used as the basis for printing.

Text can be shot through the process camera without the screen in place. This is called line origination, and depends on your text being in a form suitable to be photographed. When this is the case you have "camera ready copy".

Most modern printing is now originated using electronic scanners. These have been developed and applied to colour printing using the four colour process, which is described below. It is possible to use the same process to produce black and white originations.

The scanner uses a high intensity laser or light beam which scans the image to be printed. The image is usually mounted on a rotating drum. In the case of transparencies the image is illuminated from behind, allowing the transparency to be scanned as it would be seen on a light-box for example. Prints can also be scanned, but in this case the print is illuminated by light shining on to the print.

Because a drum is used to mount the transparency or print they must obviously be flexible. No problem as far as straightforward repro-duction is concerned; however, if you have produced a composite image and other material to be printed then it too must be flexible enough to go onto the drum. For example, a painting on board cannot be scanned using this method. Some scanners work from flat artwork, but may only produce black and white. The size of originals which these scanners can cope with can be limited as well.

The light beam feeds signals into a computer system which in turn passes electronic signals to an exposing laser. This dims and brightens according to the signal it receives and produces a screened film positive or separation on another drum. Final image sizes can be accommodated by altering the size of the drum.

The computer allows many electronic manipulations of the image such as contrast enhancement and dye-deficiency masking. The comput-er may also be programmed to provide the desired screen dot density. It is possible to see the effects of these manipulations by linking the com-puter to a visual display unit (VDU).

In comparison with a process camera the scanning process provides a faster means of producing screened film for printing, and can produce superior quality. The faithfulness of the origination to the image to be printed is under computer control, whereas when using a process cam-era such fidelity could only be gained by retouching the film.

Colour printing relies on four separations being produced in different colours: magenta, cyan, yellow and black. This combination allows for practically the full range of colours to be reproduced. For example, pur-ple is obtained by mixing certain amounts of magenta and cyan. If only the three true colours were used the results would be rather anaemic, hence the use of black to give body and fine detail to the final result.

Certain colours do not reproduce well using this process – typically golds, deep blues, and certain greens.

The scanners usually produce the four separations in parallel, making for fast, and cheap, origination. Colour densities need to be matched so that dot sizes differ according to the density of colour in the corresponding area in the original. The separations are then produced with different dot orientations, so that when the separations are placed in register with each other the different coloured dots do not lie on top of each other and do not interact to cause distracting moiré patterns.

The illusion of different colours is created by your eye's inability to resolve the fine dot clusters into individual dots. If you look through a magnifying glass at a colour picture reproduced in a book or magazine you can immediately see the dot structure.

Before leaving the topic of origination methods there are three further ones which are of interest here. The first is duotone origination. Essentially this is where two half-tone separations are produced in different colours. Often this is used for quality black and white printing, and the two separations are black and white. One may have fine highlight detail down to mid-tone values, whilst the other may be more contrasty, and go from mid-tones to shadows. It is possible to vary the nature of the two separations, and their colour, such that a wide range of black and white effects becomes achievable. Using this type of origination a full range of rich tones can be printed – at greater cost of course.

The second type of origination is line and tone. This is a separation produced from a combination of two films, one line, the other halftone. This process is used where text is to appear superimposed on a photograph, for example.

The third type is electronic page makeup, which is beginning to make an impact now. The systems using this kind of origination can scan and then store separation information on a computer hard disk. In addition, text can be stored along with graphics. Subsequently this information can be retrieved and used to produce complete pages containing several transparencies etc. These systems also allow features like airbrushing, vignetting and colour correction to be carried out with relative ease. The potential for book publishing is obvious.

The image source

Despite advances in modern origination and printing technology, which have greatly aided the reproduction of colour photographs, it is still important to provide an appropriate original.

In black and white particularly it can be difficult to achieve the full tonal range and densities achievable on photographic paper. A black and white print for reproduction should be more restricted in its tonal content than one intended for exhibition printing. Ideally, good separation of mid-tones and no large areas of pure black or pure white are the order of the day. In general therefore, it is probably best if your prints are not too contrasty – but neither should they be flat and grey.

In colour, transparencies are preferred because they are reproducible to a higher quality standard than prints, giving a brighter, sharper result. With advances in printing technology and usage this may change, especially with many newspapers using colour print originals now. However, transparencies do tend to show greater colour saturation and fidelity over prints in the majority of cases. The medium you choose to submit for printing will depend on the effects you are trying to obtain.

It is a good idea to try to keep the size of the original in keeping with the size of the eventual reproduction. For example, in my experience the reproduction of postcards (standard size 6x4in) from transparencies is impressive. On the other hand if I was publishing a book using prints, where the final reproduced image size was to be, say 7x5in, I would not supply the printing house with 16x12in enlargements. It would be better, and cheaper, to supply 7x5in prints. Doing this means less adjustments, with the attendant potential loss in quality, need be made by the printer.

In general it is sensible to supply your best originals for reproduction; duplicate slides reproduce less well. Transparencies should have detail in the highlights, even if the shadows block up. Colour images which have an overall cast could be corrected, but at the expense of general tone and colour accuracy.

Prints should generally have a glossy finish, as these reproduce better. Lustre and stipple finishes may interfere with the screening process. Remember that prints should be unmounted so they can be wrapped round the scanning drum.

Although it is possible for damaged and poorly photographed originals to be corrected during scanning, it is expensive, and it is far preferable to present a good original image to the printing process in the first place.

Proofing

Once your image has been separated a proof can be produced for your inspection by the reproduction house. Commercial printers which specialise in business printing such as brochures or company postcards will probably offer a choice of black and white proofs or colour Cromalins.

The black and white proofs are not much more than a photocopy of the separations, which show enough to tell you whether they are in register, and that the originator has understood your instructions regarding the position of the image in relation to the final product such as a postcard. This proof will also show any text, and its position, and the type style and size it is in. In short you get a lot of useful information, but very little about final print quality, and none at all regarding the way colour will reproduce in the print run.

Cromalins will give you full colour information, but will cost extra. The Cromalin system consists of a sheet of white board laminated with an ultra-violet sensitive layer. The separation is exposed onto it, and the exposed image is coloured with a colour toner. This is done for all four colours in the four colour process. A colour bar is included so that you can check registration, colour density, dot gain (more of which below) and grey balance.

A system from a different manufacturer is called the Matchprint system; it produces a similar result but uses coloured film rather than toner to achieve it.

A third type of proof is called a wet proof. If only one or two proofs are required this method is more expensive than the Cromalin process. If more than a small number of proofs are needed of the same image (not usually the case for our purposes) then wet proofs can be cheaper than Cromalins.

Wet proofs are made by producing a printing plate from the separations, then printing the image on a proofing press using the actual ink and paper that will be used during the final printing. This method has the advantage of producing a proof virtually identical to the final product, both in terms of colour balance and "feel", dependent on the paper used being the same for proof and print.

Other types of proof you may come across, especially if you are concerned with book publishing, are scatter proofs and page proofs. Scatter proofs are produced from a number of originals, masked to size, and fitted on to a proof sheet. They do not include type and are not laid out in the correct position relative to each other. Their main advantage is cheapness.

Page proofs include type and show a page as it would appear in the final print run.

You may also come across ozalids. These are inexpensive proofs of a whole book. Their appearance is similar to an architect's blueprint because they are produced by a dye-line process. Therefore they are no good for checking how your images will be reproduced, but they are very useful for determining the accuracy of the book's layout. This is especially true if you have asked for the proofs to be supplied folded and cut, so they appear in the same order and orientation as they would in the finished book. They can be used in conjunction with scatter proofs where cost is important.

With the advent of electronic systems the proofing systems of the future will be linked directly to scanners, or page makeup systems, using digital storage and transmission. Such direct digital colour proofing (DDCP) makes use of digital writers to output, via computer control, to paper utilising liquid colours. Control of dot gain, density, colour, etc. is achieved by commands to the computer.

Proof checking

It is essential that the proof be checked carefully for flaws, and for correct registration if more than one separation is to be used in the printing process. If not, mistakes left uncorrected at this stage will lead to costly adjustments later.

In essence you are looking for quality, sizing and positioning in the proof, plus colour density and balance if this is relevant. It is not always possible to match these completely to the final printed appearance for a variety of reasons, principally dot gain and paper, but a good idea can be gained from them.

Ideally the proof should be as close as possible to the final printed result, but Cromalins for colour postcards cost far more than basic black and white proofs, so you may decide the latter are adequate for your purposes.

Designers would probably check proofs using standardised lighting conditions and a densitometer, but you would need to know what you are doing before these results mean anything. The important thing to bear in mind is whether the proof looks as if you will get the result you want.

You should always carefully check the registration of the separations. Out of register separations will show in colour fringing and loss of definition. Size, trim and whether the image is bled to the edges of the card or page, or whether there is a gutter or border around it, should be as you ordered. If you have specified a gutter make sure this is the correct width. Examine type for broken, missing or illegible bits, and check whether the correct type style and size has been used. Make sure images have not been reversed by mistake, and that the colour is acceptable.

It is also possible to get a good visual feel for various printing effects at the proofing stage – all at extra cost of course. For example black and white images can be originated using the four colour process, or as a duotone by using two separations. In the latter it is often the case that one separation is a full range halftone. However it is possible to alter the second separation to introduce a tint to the black and white reproduction. Thus the second separation could be cyan, and of less intensity than the first separation which used black as its colour. In this way a blue tint can be given to a black and white reproduction whilst retaining quality. Duotones for photographic books often use pale grey as a second colour; the quality attainable can be extremely high.

Proofs can be utilised to explore a range of effects, although discussion with the printer beforehand will help keep the expense to a minimum.

Making corrections

If you have any doubts about the proof it is best to voice them at this stage. It need not be necessary to use technical language, provided you are clear about what it is that troubles you.

So, for example, the highlights in your proof may seem lacklustre. This could be due to the highlight dots being too big, thus making whites appear slightly grey. However, you should communicate your concern about the highlight areas to the printer in terms of the finished result, rather than in terms of dot size. There could be a number of technical reasons for weak highlights, and it is better to let the printer sort them out. The key thing to remember is that if you are not satisfied with a proof then you should ask the printer to produce one that you are happy about. A poor proof could lead to a poor printed result which you may have to accept if you have passed the proof.

When indicating any corrections it is important to be as clear as possible; ambiguous comments can make matters worse. You imagine you instructed the printer to do one thing, and the printer imagines you have asked for something else. The result is complete dissatisfaction with additional cost and time delays to boot.

For example, asking the printer to brighten the colours could mean lighten the colours, add more colour, or increase the contrast. Where possible direct the printer to specific procedures to achieve what you want, or discuss it at length until you are sure the printer understands the effect you are trying for.

If the proof is not up to scratch then corrections can be made. Of course, if the corrections are due to you changing your mind about how you want the image to appear, or where you want the type to be, then you will be charged for the alterations. But if the proof isn't right because the printing house hasn't done its job then they should bear the cost of reproofing – producing another proof.

Reproofing should be done if there are any major corrections to the proof. The printers may even rescan or retouch the image in order to correct it.

Printers work to a particular standard which ensures that, for example, the colours of the process inks do not vary from printer to printer. In Britain, therefore, you should expect that colours will be the same whoever you ask to print your job. If, however, you get proofs from a British repro house, but decide to have your job printed in, say, Hong Kong, then the inks used may differ. Far Eastern inks may be brighter. Although this may not be a problem, it should be borne in mind if you are in this position. It is only likely to occur if you are having a book printed elsewhere for reasons of cost.

Very often you will be able to find a printer who will take a lot of the technicality of printing out of the equation for you. So all you need do is specify the paper and how you wish the printed image to appear. As I have shown, however, it is not always possible to specify the finished product exactly for technical reasons. Understanding these reasons will help you to pre-visualise what kind of images and type of product is possible.

Two further aspects of printing need to be mentioned in this context. These are screen size and dot gain. Both of these are related to origination, proofing, and final print.

Screen size and dot gain

Colour and black and white halftone originations are made using a screen between the original image and the separation, so that the origination is made up of dots in different densities and colours. The eye cannot resolve these dots at normal viewing distances and magnifications, thus giving the illusion of continuous tone reproduction.

The dots are produced by using a screen with a grid of ruled lines, and the number of lines per inch gives the screen ruling number. It is possible to produce dots which are not square in shape, as they would be with a standard grid. Dot shapes can be round or elliptical as well.

The size of the dot is a function of the screen ruling. The finer the ruling, the finer the dot, and therefore the finer the detail that can be reproduced in the print. Common screen rulings are 300, 200, 150, 120, 100, 85, and 65 lines per inch, 300 being the finest in this series.

So why not just specify the finest screen ruling possible? Because the finest screen is not necessarily the one for the job. This is due to "dot gain" and the paper to be used in the printing.

Dot gain is the increase in the size of the dot produced by the processes intervening between the original image and the final print. It is the difference in size between the dot size used in the origination and that on the printing paper. This gain can be produced by a variety of factors including the plate making process and the paper used. The effect of dot gain is to increase colour richness because a greater area of colour is being printed than is wanted. The other main effect is that definition is reduced because when the dot size increases on the printed paper, dots can run into one another.

A major factor in dot gain is the type of paper used for printing. Quality art paper does not absorb ink in the way that less good paper, like newsprint, does. Dot gain is much bigger with newsprint since the ink is absorbed and therefore spreads over a wider area, rather like when a liquid is mopped up by a paper tissue. When the dot gain is large the screen rulings should be much less fine in order to get the best result. A coarse screen means that there are less dots in any given area, and therefore they have less chance of spreading into each other, muddying definition and colour.

Newsprint might use typically 65 or 85 screen to cope with the dot gain due to the absorbent paper. With this type of paper and screen ruling it is difficult to get good tonal range and definition. Commercial printing using coated paper for business flyers could use a screen ruling of, say, 150, because the coated paper will not absorb the ink in the way newsprint does. The ink sits more on the surface. This means it is possible to print good highlights with good definition. If the printing is on very high quality, smooth paper then a screen as high as 300 could be used. Some photographic books are made in this way.

Proofs also vary in the gain they introduce, with Cromalins, for example, producing around twice as much gain as wet proofs.

When proofing therefore, it is important to have the proof made on a paper as close as possible to the final printing paper in order to judge the definition, colour and quality to be expected from the printing house. You may need to specify this.

Some printers will produce a whole package for you so that you do not need to be concerned with intermediate aspects like screens and dot gain in relation to the paper used. In this case you lose discretion over the process in exchange for an easy life, so it is important to look at examples of past work to examine whether what the printing house will do for you meets your requirements. I have produced postcards successfully using this approach.

Paper

There are many different types of paper, from newsprint to high quality art paper. Paper can be coated or uncoated, matt or glossy, and of various weights. Printers will supply samples for you to look at. If you hire a designer he or she should be able to inform you of the most suitable types.

Weight is usually quoted in grams per square metre (gsm). Postcards, for example are printed on heavyweight card, around 300 to 350 gsm, which is treated on one side so that the image will reproduce well. The weight of the card will affect the shelf life of the product – lighter cards get damaged more easily and curl more readily as they absorb moisture. Heavy card gives a more upmarket feel which can be important for some markets, but naturally will probably cost more. Greetings cards are similar in this respect to postcards.

Posters might well be reproduced on 150 gsm art paper, although fine art prints could be on heavier paper such as 300 gsm. You can therefore get some idea of what different paper weights feel like by looking at and handling products already on the market. In addition many printing houses will provide samples for you to examine.

Of course, you can expect a designer to be able to explain and show you the various papers and their effects when images are reproduced on them.

It is worth repeating that the use of fine quality paper allows the use of very fine screens which have the potential for fine detail and tone reproduction. If you are not aiming for this standard of reproduction then the paper quality may be of less concern. Only you can decide.

Printing

Once all the proofs have been checked and returned to the printers the product can be printed. It is sometimes possible to be present when this is being done, so if you have the chance you should be there to watch your images roll off the line in final printed form.

There is a benefit to this other than the pleasure of seeing your work in print, which is that you are on hand if any last-minute printing decisions need to be made. For example the printer may not be able to set the machine to give just the colour you expect, and a compromise will have to be reached. If you are there you can influence the nature of the compromise rather than leave it to the printer to make it for you.

Printers usually print on large sheets of paper. If you are having, say, four postcards printed, then it is likely that there will be 28 other cards on the same sheet belonging to someone else. This is one way printers can offer good rates on printing small numbers of cards. But it also means that it is not always possible to insist that your requirements should be paramount when the printer needs to reach an acceptable compromise for all images on the sheet. Nonetheless by being *in situ* you can at least influence the decision-making process and hence the final outcome.

If you are not present at the printing stage then you need to check the printed result carefully when you take delivery of it. Watch out for any blemish in the final result that mars it significantly. For example, little "hickies" such as black spots with a white border, or a colour cast, or flecks of colour such as magenta in an otherwise blue sky – all are faults in printing which detract from the final result.

Another thing to look for, especially over a long run, is colour changes due to inking variation. This is something which affects offset lithography where the ink/water balance can change during the printing process. Also check that the cards or posters etc. have been properly trimmed so that their edges are clean cut and square.

These flaws could matter a great deal as far as your sales are concerned. So, although it may be very tiresome, it is essential to go through each print run looking for flaws and rejecting anything not up to your standard. Rejects should be returned to the printers and either be replaced by them, or some satisfactory arrangement reached regarding compensation.

CHAPTER CHECKLIST

● Have you decided what it is you want to produce?
● Have you decided on the "look" of your product?
● Do you know what price products like the ones you intend to market are selling for?
● Can you produce the same quality at the same price as your competitors?
● Have you obtained quotes on costs from different printers?
● Have you studied printers' sample packs of the type of printing service on offer?
● Have you got a realistic idea of the quantity of product you want to print? Remember: don't print too much.
● Are you giving value for money, but making a profit on your costs?
● Does your product design complement your image or overwhelm it?
● Have you created a design mock-up?
● Have you tested your product on retailers and distributors?
● Do you appreciate the limitations of what a printer can do for you?
● Have you supplied your best originals for reproduction?
● Have you checked the proof carefully for flaws?
● Have you made sure that you've indicated any corrections on the proof as clearly as possible?
● Have you considered the paper quality you need?
● Can you be present to watch your images roll off the printing press in their final form?
● Have you checked the printed result carefully on delivery?
● Have you rejected any print which has any blemish?

4 Marketing

This chapter is about marketing – what it is, and what needs to be considered when drawing up a marketing profile of your self-publishing activities.

Marketing can be a difficult idea to get across to those who have no experience of it. In particular the whole idea of marketing can be aversive to a person whose main interest is in producing art. The idea and language of "the product", "the market", "added value", "advertising", "range diversification", "follow-up" and so on can be seen as somehow sullying the purity of artistic vision and the reason for producing the images in the first place.

Business or hobby?

There is a real difference, therefore, between people who are freelancing as a creative hobby, and those who want to make a worthwhile profit from their activities. I shall expand on this in the following sections, but suffice it to say here that even the pure hobbyist should be considering how to cover costs, and possibly pay for equipment and materials. It is an expensive form of self-gratification if your self-publishing ventures make a loss.

It is eminently feasible, of course, to start as a hobbyist, producing and self-publishing your own work, and then to graduate to the point where this activity makes enough money to provide the option of moving up a stage to form a freelance business – though one still capable of sustaining considerable involvement in the creative side.

My advice to the hobbyist, however, would be to start by considering the range of activity you might end up with and to be clear-eyed about the initial marketing strategy. If you want to generate sufficient profit to fund future self-publishing ventures, then it will pay to be businesslike right from the start. At the very least the hobbyist should be thinking about generating realistic returns on the cost and time investment necessary to create images worthy of self-publication.

I will have more to say on what constitutes realism in the section on pricing. But for the person already committed to freelancing as a way of earning a living or producing a supplementary income, marketing is central to his or her business.

Marketing is about producing a strategy for creating the possibility of sales rather than about the selling itself, although obviously it does form the basis of your selling efforts. It is necessary, therefore, to develop a marketing plan, even though this plan may be very rudimentary when starting out.

Identifying your market

The basic idea behind marketing is that your self-publishing venture should begin by identifying what a chosen group of customers' needs and wants are, and what values they have. Your venture should then be directed at meeting those needs and wants by providing benefits.

This approach – producing what your market requires – will not undermine your creativity and it does not mean that you cannot be an artist, but it does emphasise that you are aiming to produce something which has a market of some sort. It is this market which needs to be identified.

The market can be taken at a very general level. There is an enormous market for postcards and greeting cards for example. Appraising the extent of the market at this scale will give you an idea of the total worth of a market, even if you are going to be concerned with but a small part of it. It will also give you an idea of your total market share, and the possibilities for future expansion. Importantly, you will need to set marketing objectives, and these too may relate to the total market in which you hope to operate.

However, this broad appraisal will not lead to direct market activity.

Thus to say that there is a good market for photographic books is obviously true, but not very helpful. You would not know what type of book to produce. What is needed is clearer market appreciation on your part. So the photographic book market could be split into "how to" books on techniques or creativity, monographs (usually by already famous photographers), and "theme" books, for example on gypsies or on a concept like "birth".

Similarly, the poster market can be classified into humorous, romantic or fine art categories, amongst others. Postcards can be straight or arty or moody, and so on. The point is that these different categories may attract different buyers and may – indeed almost certainly will – need different marketing objectives, plans and strategies.

Market segmentation

It is therefore vital to have an idea of the different ways of segmenting a market. The most common ones are in terms of demographic, geographic and individual factors.

Demographic factors are those concerning populations. For example they include age, sex, occupation, religion, nationality, income and social class. Geographic factors basically consider the market from the point of view of location, for example cities, counties, tourist resorts and countries.

Individual factors are related to much more personal characteristics and lifestyle – feminine, masculine, independent, yuppie, single, married and so on. Included in this category would be user status – that is whether buyers are first-time, regular or impulse, and user level – that is whether they purchase a lot or a little when they buy. For example the poster market is characterised by purchasers who buy the occasional poster, whereas postcards might attract regular, heavy buyers. View postcards are going to appeal to both tourists and locals, but the former group may buy the most.

Segmenting the market in this way will give you a much better idea of your potential customers, the people for whom you are making your product. It will help you identify which products are likely to do well in which market and whether you are able to meet particular niche market needs. Thus you will be able to decide whether to try and cover several market segments or concentrate on only one or two.

In essence, recognising the market and your ability to provide for it allows you to target those segments where you are most likely to succeed. Analysing markets is a time-consuming task, but resist the temptation simply to make your product and take it to market. You are most likely to end up with a lot of product and few sales, which can turn out to be very expensive.

Market research

Market research is concerned with finding out about the needs and wants of your market and whether your product or products will genuinely meet them. It is about gaining information before spending large sums of money and committing resources to production which may not sell. It is therefore important for any business. It cannot eliminate business risk, but it can help to reduce it if properly done.

There are several stages to doing this research. These include: deciding what information is needed; determining the sources from whom the information should be gathered; deciding on the questions to be put to them; considering how to sample the sources so that a proportion of them will be able to provide a good picture of them all; planning the questioning process; conducting the enquiries; analysing the answers.

If you were researching the potential for a range of postcards of a particular locality, then clearly you would restrict your research to that locality. Next you would decide how you were going to sell. Just through local shops, or are you going to include direct selling using advertising? If it is just shops you could get a list of local retailers from the Chamber of Commerce or from the local Yellow Pages.

Next you need to pick the shops you think will appeal to your target market. Now you have a decision to make. How many of the shops will you visit for research purposes? If only a small number exist you could visit them all. Otherwise you will have to sample them, especially if your time is limited and you need answers quickly.

Sampling techniques

Deciding on a sample is a key process which should be done carefully, according to established principles. If you do not pick a representative sample you will end up with a distorted picture of the market potential of your product. If you get the sampling right you will save time and money as well as obtain an accurate appreciation of the market.

So what are the established sampling techniques? Three are potentially relevant to the self-publisher. First is random sampling. All the retailers in your area have an equal chance of being chosen. To do this you could use random number tables, or put all the names of the shops into a hat and draw them out. This technique is thought to give very accurate results.

Second, you could take a systematic sample, such as every fifth retailer in a list. Third, you can stratify your sample. If you are aiming to produce postcards of the "arty" type then sampling standard newsagents could be a waste of time, and concentrating on "art" outlets would be more representative of your potential market. You should still include some ordinary newsagents though, because you are trying for an accurate picture of the total market, and your decision to concentrate on "art" shops might miss a marketing opportunity. But your sample should naturally be biased to the outlets you consider to have more potential.

Next the questions you are going to ask have to be decided upon. There are two possible lines of enquiry. First you can simply ask what the likes and dislikes of your potential customers are, in order to get a customer profile. Second you can take your product (or a mock up) along and ask about its potential in that selling environment. I have done the latter and found it worked very well.

The guiding principle for the kinds of question to ask is whether it tells you what you want to know. For example, "will this product appeal to your (the retailer's) customers?", "would the you stock it, and in what quantities?", "is there a seasonal element in your sales?", "what are your customers' preferences and are you satisfied with current products on the market?", "how would you display it?", and so on.

It is a good idea to be conversational rather than simply interrogating the retailer. Also, be flexible. New questions may occur to you as you go along. However, it is a good idea to ask a set of standard questions in a fixed order so all the shops answer the main points under similar conditions and you can make a fairer comparison between them. Thus having your questions on a clipboard is a good idea, and looks professional as well.

Aside from face to face interviewing, you could consider asking questions over the telephone. This saves time, but changes the nature of the conversation. A good telephone manner is essential. Another disadvantage is that your interviewee cannot see your mock-up.

An alternative is to post questionnaires to your sample retailers. Again this is time saving, although the costs of postage and producing the questionnaires should not be forgotten. Also, a common problem with postal questionnaires is that they are all too easily chucked in the bin, so you get only a small proportion back. 40% or less is a typical expectation for a response rate. Thus your market picture could be heavily distorted.

You may meet with some retailers who are too busy or won't cooperate for some other reason. You will have to accept this if you can't persuade them otherwise. After all they don't have to take part. I have found that most retailers are willing to join in though, especially if interested in the product; they recognise another small business person like themselves.

If you do get dropouts your sample may suffer and you may lose some accuracy in the marketing picture you obtain. Thus when you evaluate the results of your research you will need to bear this in mind. Usually it won't be too serious.

Once you have the answers to your questions it is time to analyse them carefully. Central to this process is the point of the whole exercise: Is there enough demand of the right sort for my kind of product, or a product I could make?

Whichever way you summarise this, do it methodically and objectively.

It is too easy to overlook answers which tell you things you don't want to hear. Try and get numbers down so that you have an idea of the sales potential. Simply finding out that your product is liked is encouraging, but tells you nothing about future income or what quantity of product to make.

Once you have a general picture of the market, test it out if you can by getting another opinion from someone active in the market, such as a producer or a friend in a similar line.

Targeting the buyer

It is a good idea to evaluate your strengths and weaknesses in relation to your chosen market segment. Assess the opportunities you have – to fill a gap in the market for example – and consider the threat to your activities from competitors. Your analysis should concentrate on the needs, wants and desires of your target group and the benefits you and your competitors are offering in order to meet them.

How on earth does this marketing-speak apply to creative visual products, I hear you ask?

Well, if you are in the postcard market then the tangible benefit you are supplying is a means of communication. This could be a simple "Hello, I was here" message. A straightforward view postcard will meet this need.

However, people who are more visually aware may want to get that element across when sending a card, and their need can only be met by a creative image. Thus your stunning image, shot at dawn, with lovely lighting, offers an intangible benefit to that buyer.

Products are often comprised of both tangible and intangible benefits. These will often be of varying importance, depending on the type of person doing the buying. Your market position will depend on how well you meet the market's needs compared to the competition.

Having an insight into the type of person who will buy your product will help you produce the products they will buy. Thus try to form a view of who your customer is in terms of their environment, family, age, income, status, culture, work and leisure pursuits. You are after as complete a picture as possible so that you can predict their needs and wants, and hence their buying behaviour. This will lead to more informed decisions about what type of product to make, how many you are likely to sell, what type of sales outlet you are likely to sell in, and the best way to promote your products.

The next stage in formulating your marketing plan is to consider the marketing mix. This consists of deciding on the product or products you are going to sell, settling on a price or prices, including special rates and discounts, promoting the product, and choosing how to distribute it to sales outlets.

Decisions of quantity

If you are just starting out on the freelance road then you may only have one product. One postcard on its own would be unlikely to sell though, primarily because you have to persuade retailers to stock it. It would mean they need to go through the process of clearing display space for your product and setting up payment procedures centred round just one item – hardly worth their while.

True, I have known a case of one card comprising the sole product line of a freelance photographer, but he was exceptional, and the card was not a standard location image but a picture of a woman's lips. The card sold, and the photographer broke even on production costs. However the time and sales effort involved did not match the reward, and there was no follow up.

This is the time to think in terms of a range, or a number of cards which have similar production values and which hang together as a group. Around eight cards would be a sensible quantity to begin with, although it would be possible to get away with less. Fewer than four would not give the impression of a set.

If you look at what the opposition is doing you will get an idea of the ranges on offer from your future competitors.

One poster image, on the other hand, is much more acceptable since the buyer will be unlikely to be collecting posters in the way postcards are bought. Posters are much more likely to be viewed and purchased singly. This is true of greetings cards too. And naturally one book is all you are likely to start with!

Product life

How ever you begin, there are some things to consider. The first is that your product will have a limited life in the marketplace. This differs for different markets. Postcards, for example, can go on selling for a very long time, whereas posters can be very subject to fashion, unless the image is a classic. Books will tend to have a lengthy shelf life. It all depends on the market you are in, and the appeal of your product.

Nonetheless it is important to realise that buying decisions are influenced by things other than just the quality of the image. So you may have a favourite picture, and it could be outstanding, but it will still have a limited sales appeal over time. This means you should be constantly appraising and reappraising your market, and planning on what you will bring to the market next.

Products, therefore, are in one of three states: they are either new on the market, in a mature phase, or declining (in terms of sales).

New products will probably sell well initially because of novelty, but you have money tied up in them as you will have only just manufactured them. Mature products which meet a market need should still be selling well on their own merits while you should by now have recouped the production costs, so they are bringing in steady money for you and profitability is high. Declining products are past their peak sales potential. The rate of sales is falling, and they may soon become less attractive for the retailer to stock since space will be wanted for faster moving items.

Thus try to think in terms of the life-span of a product as a matter of course; it will help stave off disappointment when it is time to take your favourite off the market. When one product is declining in sales then a new line should be waiting in the wings.

You should also be keeping an eye on what your competitors are doing. You may find a retailer unwilling to stock your products because they are selling more slowly than those of your competitors.

Getting ideas for new products and images should be part of your activities, but don't overlook the market research that may be needed for any new line.

Producing a range

The above underlines the value of the idea of a range of products, and from the marketing point of view there are several additional advantages to thinking in terms of a range other than merely continued selling as mentioned above.

Firstly, a range means you give the customer some choice in their purchasing decisions. So, for example, if a buyer likes your greetings card aimed at the "get well soon" market, their natural urge is to look for other cards you produce, and select the best one according to taste. This is a psychological aspect of buying which may lead to more sales than if you have only the one type of greetings card on offer. Bear in mind though, that too much choice can be counter-productive.

Secondly, a range reinforces the elements within it. A set of cards

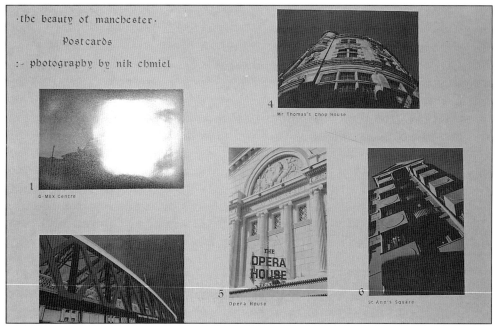

·the beauty of manchester·

Postcards

:- photography by nik chmiel

My "marketing board". I use this board to gather reactions from potential retailers to my postcard range. Their responses help me to decide how many images to include in the range and in what type of retail outlet the range would sell well. The original board uses colour photographs, of course.

which all share the same production values will highlight those values, leading to greater buying confidence and hence more sales.

But it is important to only include cards or whatever if they have this reinforcing nature. Chucking in any old image just to get the numbers up could destroy the overall projection of the range to the buyer, even if they like the other cards. If you find this to be the case after you have started selling, you should seriously consider pulling the offending card out of your line rather than leave it to build up a negative impression.

In addition a range means the customer may buy two cards rather than one, thus increasing your sales without any further effort on your part. That is extremely cost effective.

It is a sad fact of marketing life that not all your products will sell. You may find yourself in the position of having, for example, two or three postcards which do extremely well, but several which, for one reason or another, stay on the shelves. If you are offering a good range it is relatively straightforward to drop the cards that are selling less well and replace them with others. But if you only have one or two on the market it soon becomes obvious if a card is not selling, which does not engender confidence in the mind of the retailer, or in the buying public.

Of course if you have an accurate picture of your target consumer group you will also have a clear idea of their needs, and will have produced a product to meet them. Getting an accurate picture is the difficult part though, and may well prove impossible without testing the market first, despite the advice given above. Unless you have access to extensive market research you will simply have to rely on gut feel plus a few judicious soundings.

Being prepared for some failures is far more realistic than believing all your products will be a sure-fire success. You will be doing well if most of your cards are meeting your sales targets.

Maintaining your range

Once you have some products on the market, have put effort into selling them, and have raised customer awareness of them, it would be a shame to waste your work by letting your range grow old and stale. You can capitalise on your profile in the market – and the expectations of your products among buyers – by introducing new ones.

After a while you may also be keen to expand your market to different consumers. This too should involve constructing additional profiles. If you are already making new wave postcards, for example, you may decide to move to a more conventional product for those less visually adventurous. Or you could go the other way and produce really far out cards for the truly trendy. Thus you could find yourself marketing several products to the same retailer, even though they may be designed for differing markets.

In practice this may not be so straightforward, because the person who counts most, the customer, may have different needs at different times. Thus the same person could end up buying products aimed at very different markets. In this case you are competing with yourself to some extent. However, the key point is that you will be selling into different markets, and your main competition will not be you, but others with products appealing to the same people you are trying to reach. How your product compares with theirs is thus a crucial factor in how well your product does.

One part of any comparison is how close the benefits your product offers comes to matching the needs of the marketplace relative to the competition. A second major part is the perceived value your product has – and a big part of that is the price you are selling it at.

1

2

3

4

Images 1—8 comprise the first postcard range of Manchester that I produced. All the cards were printed with a white border and to the same consistency in order to make them distinctive in the shops and coherent as a set. Although all these images sold well, image 8 of St Ann's Square was slow-moving and I later replaced it with image 17 (see page 74) produced in the same style.

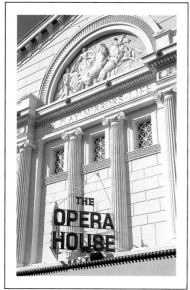

5

6

7

8

9

10

11

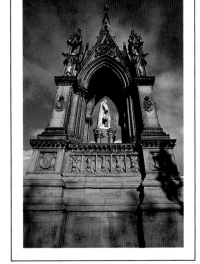

12

Images 9—16 comprise the second range of Manchester postcards I produced. I wanted to retain a continuity with the first set (images 1—8) and so these were also produced with a white border. However, I wanted them to be perceived as a different range, an addition rather than a replacement, so they were printed lighter than the first set, and used a different reverse (see page 25).

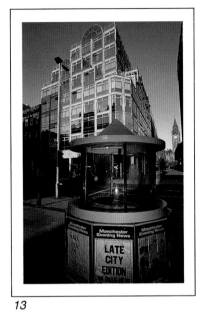

13

14

15

16

17

18—20

17—22 are all images of Manchester University. Image 17 was produced to replace image 8 in my first postcard range, and is included here as a contrast to demonstrate how different styles of photograph have their effect. Images 18—22 were all commissioned and hence produced to order. Their style reflects the requirement of the person who comissioned them, who felt that image 17 had too many converging lines. Images 18—20 all appeared on one card, which is more expensive but can be effective. Interestingly, image 17 quickly sold out!

21

22

23

24

Image 23 of St Ann's Church is included to demonstrate that although this church is well-known and a lovely building, an angular style doesn't suit such a classical subject well enough for it to sell. Image 24 demonstrates that some photographs can be plain boring and thus unlikely to sell. Compare this image to image 11. Both are detail shots of the Cathedral, but which one would you buy?

"They don't make them like they used to." I took this with a poster in mind. Posters are a mixture of image and text which work best if they illustrate a mood, or humour, or a concept. They are destined to be on display for a considerable time, unlike most postcards, therefore they should stand prolonged scrutiny. This image was take on a 5x4in camera to ensure that tone and colour as well as detail could be retained when enlarged to poster size. The mood I was aiming for was predominantly nostalgia, which is why I left the dry leaves on the floor.

"Still Waters." This is another image taken with a 5x4in camera and intended for poster reproduction. The same considerations as for the previous image apply, although the mood intended here is *"peace and away from it all."*

Pricing

The price of a product is a very important aspect of its marketing. Most markets are price sensitive. If you are new to the market your product's price will be largely determined by what is already there, whereas if you are already a well-known name in your field you may be able to influence price and be the market leader – or at least a price pacesetter.

The price is not, of course, simply determined by the makers and retailers of the product, but also by what people are prepared to pay. Thus postcards, for example, have a "price ceiling" above which the general public won't willingly go. Postcards are seen to be a cheap, easy way of sending a message to someone else. Added value is hard to come by.

Greetings cards on the other hand, have a much greater scope. Valentine cards can cost several times a simple "get well soon" card. Thus the same image produced as a postcard will earn less than if it appears on a greetings card, other things being equal.

It is easy to see, therefore, that setting a price is a function of perceived value and not just dependent on manufacturing costs. Nevertheless the latter is central to establishing the price your product should sell at.

The price you get for your product naturally has to cover the production costs of making it, for example the printing costs, and also the costs involved in creating the imagery – the film and processing costs, your time costs in terms of taking photographs, attending to business matters, and marketing and selling the product. Each market and product will have a different equation comprising these elements. If you have no experience of the market then you can get some idea by looking at what's selling and working backwards.

Thus if a postcard sells at 25p, work on the assumption that the retailer bought it for 12p. The difference – the retailer's mark-up – covers overheads like renting the premises, heating and lighting, plus profit. This means you have to make your card for 12p or less.

A rule of thumb some people consider sensible is that you should add 100% to your production costs when selling on. Therefore you would need to make the card for 6p and sell it to the retailer for 12p. 100% is probably a conservative margin, and a more appropriate one could be as high as 200% in order to cover other expenses and still make a profit to pay yourself and fund future product development.

One further point is that unless your turnover is very considerable (see chapter 7) you will not be registered for VAT. Therefore the price you sell at to the retailer should recognise this. That is, the retailer will most likely be VAT registered, and if so will have to add VAT to your price as well as their own profit margin before arriving at the retail price of your product.

Managing your costs

It is important, then, to try and itemise all the costs that bear on bringing your card to market and to calculate a unit cost for them. These fall roughly into four areas: materials, overheads, labour and profit.

Materials includes the monies involved in actually making the product. Thus your film, processing, designing, printing and packaging costs should be reckoned up. Overheads are the costs associated with running your business. This includes telephone bills, paperwork and travelling expenses. Labour costs are those related to the time you spend in bringing the product to market, and profit includes what you decide to allow for future business activity.

You should calculate these costs for a fixed period of time, say a month, or six months, or even a year. This will give you a figure per card that you have to recoup over your accounting period in order to produce the profit you have allowed for in your costings. Do not sell at loss if you can possibly avoid it. You are in business. If you want to offer discounts in order to encourage sales then make sure you have worked the discount structure into your costings.

In the postcard market you will quickly discover that the manufacturing cost per card goes down if you have a large number of cards printed. However if the market is already full of competitors, and your product has a shortish life, you may end up sitting on a large number of unsold cards. This means that those you have sold need to recoup your costs.

Deciding in advance on what will sell is very difficult, especially without prior experience, and it may be better to keep the initial print run down and hope to sell every card, and then print more later. This means each card will be more expensive to produce – that is, the unit cost will be higher. If possible it would then be a good idea to increase the perceived value of your card and so charge a higher price.

Adding value

The perceived value of "arty" or "new wave" postcards is much higher than the traditional, standard view card. The differences are in the quality of the images in terms of their creativity and use of mood, and in the production values utilised. Higher production values are seen, for example, in the use of white borders around the image, or in the addition of stylised type on the card front.

Very often the adoption of higher values need not increase the cost by much. That is, the marginal cost is low for the potential gain in your selling price to the retailer. Thus new wave cards are generally sold at a much higher price than traditional cards, typically 35p to 40p at present. Thus if the retailer marks up by 100% you can sell to them for 18p to 20p, whilst producing for, say, 8p. It is probable that this type of card will not sell in the sort of quantities that cheaper cards do, and probably not in as many outlets, but this won't matter if you are a small producer.

The notion of added value is therefore important to the self-publisher because of the relatively small scale of the operation. Big companies can take advantage of economies of scale to keep prices low, so the self-publisher will find it very difficult to compete on price alone.

Other ways to add value could include keeping the product exclusive, or making it different in the marketplace. For example, oversize postcards can have added perceived value compared to the standard size.

Reducing overheads

Pricing inevitably implies cost considerations, and you should look at your way of doing things to check whether your costs are being minimised, or whether you are wasting money.

To the person who is freelancing whilst holding down another job this can seem difficult to do, and perhaps somewhat pointless. After all, the marginal expenses of the additional activity do not appear high. For example if you use your car to deliver postcards to your local retailer, all you seem to be doing is using a bit of petrol. You own the car anyway and are doing the delivery in your spare time.

However another way of looking at it is that your journey to the retailer costs more than just the petrol. It includes wear and tear on the car, and you couldn't make the trip if you had not got insurance, tax and an MOT, all of which cost money. Then there is the time you spend in the car and making the delivery, and as they say, time is money.

So really you should be paying yourself for your work as a freelance. If you are running a freelance business you will certainly be thinking along the latter lines.

It is, therefore, crucial to consider all the aspects of your business activities when looking at costs, and then try to minimise your outgoings. Do not make two separate trips to sales outlets if you can combine them in one journey; do get film processed in large batches if it attracts a discount; do spend your time constructively; and do set your paperwork on a sound footing which allows easy and rapid accounting.

Handling price increases

Despite your best efforts you will probably be faced at one time or another with increases in manufacturing expenses. What do you do when your costs go up?

You will almost certainly need to raise your product price, unless you decide to absorb the increases yourself. You may judge that the latter course of action is preferable, depending on the current state of the market. But if it looks like you will be making a loss then passing the cost increases on becomes inevitable.

Many would be wary of doing so without also adding some value to the product, so that the retailers feel that they are also getting something extra for the extra money they need to pay out. Of course, if costs are rising generally, and the buying public perceive this to be the case, then there will be an expectation of price rises because a lot of prices will be going up, not just yours. The other side of this coin is that once you start charging one price for your goods it is difficult to change it without a sound reason. So if you get the pricing wrong to start with then you could be stuck with it for quite a while.

If you are undercharging you have two options: stick with it, or change it as quickly as you can after you start selling the product – but have an excuse ready for why you are doing so.

Promotion

Promotion at the marketing level is mostly to do with creating a professional image designed to help you get sales – or at least impart confidence to the retailers who buy your product. This area can be a very subtle one, in that the reasons why retailers choose to stock your particular cards or posters may be completely unpredictable. Little things may matter a great deal. It is important to get the main details which are under your control right, however. Thus the impression you convey to your clients is instrumental in your business success.

How you appear to your customers can be determined in several different ways. These include your approach when selling, your appearance, the paperwork the customer receives, and the image advertising you do.

This impression is dependent on both functional and emotional factors. The end objective is the creation of a professional image in the mind of your buyers which gives them confidence and reassures them as to your reliability. You want them to do well for you, as well as for themselves.

The initial approach to a retailer is very important. Your appearance and manner may produce a very positive response to your products, or the opposite.

The paperwork which accompanies your delivery and invoicing should convey a businesslike impression. The advent of cheap, computer-based, word-processing and graphics packages means that it is easy to produce attractive letterheads and other business stationery. These are very much more professional looking than an invoice book bought from the local stationer. And print looks much more upmarket than handwriting on statements and the like.

Distribution

Distribution in the marketing context is concerned with the way in which your product is brought to the marketplace. That is, it centres on the distribution channels through which your product is made available, rather than the physical delivery of your goods to the end user.

Distribution channels are what lie between you, the producer, and the customer. Each channel will have some procedure, and some people, involved in taking your product from you and passing it to those who will sell it to your target market. In some cases there may be no channel involved – you sell direct to the end user – but in the markets we are concerned with here, that is unusual.

There are a number of things to bear in mind when deciding on the channel to be employed. The first is the size of the market, and how spread out it is. For example, if you are producing view postcards of your local area then sales will be confined to that locale, and distribution will be through local newsagents. However if you are producing greetings cards then you need a distribution chain which gets your cards into as many appropriate shops in the country as possible.

Second, the nature of your product will influence the distribution needed. Fine art posters will likely appear in different trade catalogues to posters with a shorter life span, like some of the humorous ones. Products with different handling requirements will be distributed accordingly. Books are vastly different to postcards. A bookshop will order perhaps one or two items, whereas postcards could be sold by the box full. And if your product is seasonal – for example, Easter or Valentine cards –

then their distribution needs a network sensitive to that aspect.

Third, the type of outlet for your product needs to be identified. Standard view postcards appear in most newsagents, while new wave cards get sold in art shops and galleries. In my experience the two don't mix readily. Your distributor should be chosen so that your product reaches your target market easily.

Fourth, consider whether you want your product to be in the same point of sale as your competitors' products. Choose a different distribution chain if you don't.

Finally, take a realistic view of the scale of your operation and trim your distribution accordingly. If you produce a few hundred postcards a year of your local area, then the best distribution is probably your own two feet and a willingness to sell to retailers who will then sell on to your target buyers. If you are producing general appeal posters, on the other hand, selling locally will get you some business, but not as much as national distribution.

The latter is fine, of course, but only if you can supply demand. Paying for a big distribution network, but only providing it with a modest quantity of product, is not very cost effective.

Distribution networks for self-published cards, posters and books include newsagents, department stores, independent bookshops, chain bookstores, art galleries, framing shops, university shops and wholesalers in the paper products market. Direct selling distribution encompasses catalogue and mail order methods, but these are unlikely to be of interest to people doing it themselves.

What the self-publisher needs to do is ascertain the share of the target market which each distribution channel has, and what future trends in distribution are around the corner. For example, newsagents may have been the place to buy postcards in the past, but with the advent of new types of card, and an increasing visual awareness on the part of the buying public, art shops could be the best outlets in the future. Also, information centres are carrying an increasing number of postcards, rather than simply supplying information, thus offering exposure to large numbers in the tourist market.

Advertising

Advertising is a relatively easy way to promote your product, but it is not easy to appreciate its benefits. This may be especially true for the self-publisher. However, a decision whether to advertise or not will depend on what product you are publishing, the size of your operation, and its extent.

For example, if you are producing postcards destined to sell locally, then advertising may be less effective than direct selling. If, on the other hand, your cards are distributed over a huge geographic region, then advertising could turn out to be the best promotional option. Nonetheless it is the case that advertising is rather indirect as a selling tool. This is because it can be quite difficult to contact your target market precisely, and there is no straightforward way of telling that a sale has resulted from an advert.

There are two kinds of advertising. First where the advertising is simply conveying product information, like how much it is, where it can be bought, what it does and so on. The second type is more concerned with image portrayal, making the public feel good about your product, or ensuring they remember it more vividly than that of your competition. In both cases the advert should be designed to attract attention and be targeted as much as possible on your identified market.

If you decide to write or design the advertising yourself then here are a few suggestions. First, keep the advertising copy simple. Use a single idea or concept, and stick to short sentences and words. Use testimonials or reviews. Second, if you think the effect is justified, use your imagery to convey what your product looks like. Place captions beneath the photograph as these are most likely to be read. Third, underline the benefits of your product, even if they appear obvious to you. Fourth, ask for a response to the advert. Put prices into it and explain where your product can be bought.

When deciding on advertising you should ask the various media – radio, newspapers, etc. – what their audience is. Local newspapers could be a very effective way to get your product message across. There are also more direct methods such as leafleting on a house-to-house basis, or having your sales literature included in the free local newspaper. It is worth remembering that a single advert may not produce much in the way of business and that an advertising campaign will probably be more effective – but of course more costly.

The main difficulty with advertising for the self-publisher is evaluating whether the cost of the advertising is worth the extra sales. It is sensible therefore, to draw up a set of objectives for your advertising. Make these specific. For example, define your target group and locale, and the time over which they will receive your advertising message. Then decide how much you are willing to spend on promotion, and what proportion of this is to be advertising.

Finally, don't expect instant results. It takes time to build product awareness in the marketplace.

CHAPTER CHECKLIST

- Have you set your business objectives?
- What are your business objectives in terms of quantity, and quality?
- What are your marketing goals?
- What is the nature of your marketplace?
- How is the market segmented?
- What are your target market's needs, wants and desires?
- How does the market perceive the benefits in your product?
- How does the market perceive the benefits in your competitors' products?
- What are your strengths and weaknesses?
- What are your competitors' strengths and weaknesses?
- Are your marketing goals realistic in relation to the opportunities and threats in the marketplace?
- Which market segment suits your strengths best and offers the best opportunities?
- What tangible and intangible benefits differentiates your product from your competitors and gives it an edge?
- How does your target market perceive value, and hence what price will the market bear?
- What distribution channels handle your product?
- Which distribution channel will give you the best chance for maximum sales?
- What promotional activities will you undertake?

5 Selling

This chapter is concerned with selling – what to sell, to whom, and how to sell. Topics considered include identifying the distribution network for your product and the customers it will sell to, selling methods, packaging, selling skills and negotiation.

Selling itself is helped considerably by good marketing, and indeed there is some overlap in the marketing and selling processes. The first part of this chapter is concerned with what products and services you will be offering and in what way. The second part will concentrate on the skills needed to increase your chances of selling, and the third part will look at how to increase your business by offering add-on products or services in addition to selling your main product.

Sales targeting

In the last chapter on marketing I talked about the various distribution channels that you could use to bring your goods to market, such as newsagents, bookshops, book wholesalers, poster shops, framing businesses, art galleries and so on. In marketing terms, there is no problem in treating these as roughly equivalent distribution means when assessing them for ways of getting your product to the marketplace – although they all differ in their effectiveness for different markets and customers. None of them involve you in direct selling to the end user.

There is a difference between them when it comes to selling however. The difference is best illustrated by the following contrast between two ways of reaching your target market.

If you self-publish a book then it is likely that the most efficient and cost effective way to distribute it is through a book wholesaler, certainly if you want country-wide exposure. To do this you arrange a contract with the wholesaler, who then becomes responsible, in part, for selling the book on to the customer. You have not actually had to sell the book to the wholesaler.

If, on the other hand, you have produced a set of postcards of your local area and you want to distribute them to local newsagents yourself, then you will be engaged in persuading the newsagents to stock your cards instead of, or alongside, those of your competitors. Your target markets are still local people and tourists, but you are effectively deploying your selling skills to convince newsagents to buy, before they sell on. There is no contract, simply a business transaction.

Whichever way you choose to distribute your product, it will help you greatly if you set selling targets. These will depend on your marketing aims and goals, and also on the means by which you achieve them. Thus your sales targets are a function of how you see yourself in marketing terms, and how much you want to earn in any period.

Earnings will be related to your selling effort. On average you may only sell something every fifth, or every third, or whatever, visit to the retailer or distributor. It follows that in order to increase sales you need to increase visits to reach the required sales volume. Having a clear idea of the visits figure will allow you to plan your time for selling and help you determine how much you could earn at best.

Selling methods

There are a number of selling methods. The ones likely to be of most concern to the freelance self-publisher are face-to-face (direct) selling, telephone selling and selling through advertising.

If you are just starting out you will probably find yourself involved in face-to-face selling, whereas once you have an established business with sufficient turnover your selling effort could include advertising and other forms of promotion, with the actual exchange of goods handled by a distributor. The choice will, of course, be yours, and it is unlikely that you would rely on one method exclusively.

The key to successful selling lies in a positive attitude to the product and the sale. Selling is not a dirty word, but is a means of bringing the benefits of your product to the customer so that their needs and wants are fulfilled. If you are uncertain about the benefits your product has, you will not convince someone else of them. Identifying benefits is part of the marketing process, and should be done before meeting or talking to potential customers. In addition you should have targeted your customers through some form of market research so that you know what their needs and wants are likely to be.

In short, you should approach the selling of your product with a clear idea of what benefits you can offer and who they suit. Take a definite view of both these aspects. Even if you are wrong in some of the detail the fact that you have made up your mind about them will help you take a confident, positive approach to your customers. Such an approach will bring sales.

A half-hearted, diffident, nervous person is not a good seller. Believe in your product! For a self-publisher this should be easy because you have already travelled a hard road to bring the product into being. If you did not believe it was worthwhile you would have given up already. Therefore don't let that belief get hidden by the prospect of selling, but use it to convey your enthusiasm for your product.

Selling points

Selling is not about giving the same spiel to all your potential buyers, but should involve taking a different approach to suit different customers.

For example, you have produced a wonderful range of postcards, with very high class imagery on them. When you approach a gallery you can appeal to their artistic standards in order to sell your cards. When you talk to a newsagent, on the other hand, you can point out the novel local scenes you have included. The point is that you need to form an opinion of each of your customers and tailor your selling to them. Remember that not all your buyers will rank the benefits of your product in the same way.

The consideration of benefits carries another important message – do not sell on price alone. When you were looking at the marketing of your product you should have decided on a price which reflected a combination of cost, perceived value and a judgement about what the market would pay for the quantities you wanted to sell. Undoubtedly price is a factor in selling, but it is only one. If you choose to stress the price of your product when trying to get a sale you are effectively saying your product has nothing else of particular interest or merit to the market.

If you have enough customers willing to buy your product, or ideally more customers than you need to meet your sales targets, then the less dependent your business can be on price.

When selling, the perceived value of your product is very important and will influence the willingness of buyers to purchase it. But this may not be the value you thought your product had when you worked out the perceived value in marketing terms.

For example, you have produced your postcards with a white border, giving each picture a frame of sorts. In the border you have printed a black keyline (a thin line going all round the image) which has added a touch of style to your cards. You therefore feel that this extra has added perceived value and hence you have set a higher price on your cards than those of the competition, which are all full bleed (the picture occupying the entire front of the card) productions.

So a retailer buys the cards from you. But not for the reason you think (which is to do with the style), but simply because that retailer wants to give his or her shop a slightly upmarket feel. The retailer, in fact, is not particularly bothered about selling the cards on, but it just suits them to keep the cards on display. Future sales to this customer are likely to suffer, and will be harder work than to a retailer who uses your added value elements to promote the cards and hence help them to sell more vigorously. Part of the problem here is that you have targeted the retailer's customers and added value for them, rather than the retailer him/herself.

Mark-ups and discounts

You will also find that, even though you are selling your cards to all retailers at the same price, they will mark them up differently, so that one outlet will be more expensive than another. This is beyond your control of course, although many retailers will ask you for a suggested retail price. In practice I have found it helps to sell postcards by giving them both the cost price and my suggested retail price, without being asked. Their final selling price will depend on their customers perception of value of that outlet.

For example, some of my postcards were selling in a chic, arty outlet for 33% more than the same cards in a students' union, but the number of cards sold did not differ significantly between the two outlets. Obviously you may alter your pricing structure to reflect this kind of final price difference, but beware you are not squeezing the more expensive retailer's profit margin, which may be the same as the less expensive outlet. The former's fixed costs may be higher, because of having a better location for example.

The key thing to take from the foregoing is that it is a bad idea to make price alone the main selling consideration. If you sell only on that basis you are begging retailers to ask questions like: "why can't it be cheaper?" or "where can I get a similar product for less", or worst of all, "if price is it, how can I bargain the price down; what is the lowest price the producer is willing to accept?"

Although the general point about pricing is sound, there is an important aspect of it which aids selling, and that is a discount structure. It is up to you whether you offer discounts on your products, but if you do the first point to make is that the discount structure should be part of your overall marketing and sales view. Do not sell at a loss. You are in business after all.

However, sensible discounting can help you sell more than you might otherwise do. It will invariably do so if you tie the discount to bulk buying on the part of your customers.

Say, for example, you are selling postcards to the local tourist information centre. This is an opportunity for you to try and persuade them to buy in bulk, because they have huge numbers of potential postcard senders making tourist enquiries during the season. It also pays you to get one large order because you then don't have to make several visits, delivering smaller quantities each time. You will save on overheads, and get money into the bank sooner. Giving a discount on large orders is the way to tempt the tourist office into giving you one.

Of course, before approaching them you will need to work out the size of the discount, and what quantity you will offer it on. One obvious method is to grade it so that the bigger the order, the larger the discount.

Packaging

The look of your product was discussed in the chapters on image and production. Here I will consider the related aspects of packaging.

Distribution – or rather the actions of your distributors – is the key to successfully selling a product. Bear in mind that your retailer will want more of your product if their customers want it, say nice things about it and ask for more of it. It helps, therefore, to make the selling job your distributor has to do easier and more rewarding.

If you can make the distributor feel good about your product into the bargain, then they will put extra effort into your product, with the likely outcome of increased sales. An effective way of achieving this is to make your product attractive, both in itself and by the packaging you use.

The first thing to do is distinguish between packaging for delivery to the distributor (including retailers), and packaging which will appear at the point of sale. Naturally it is the latter which will have the biggest impact on sales to the end customer. However, the former should not be neglected because your packaging for delivery could also influence the way you are perceived by the distributor.

For example, if you deliver your postcards in white paper bags it looks unprofessional and a bit sloppy, especially if the bags are in any way crumpled, which they might be after a car journey. Your distributor could well get the impression that you don't treat your own product very carefully, and take a similar attitude. You want your delivery packaging to promote your professional business image and engender a positive attitude from your distributors.

Some packaging can be very expensive when you are starting out, especially if you employ a commercial company to do it for you. Thus you need to think about packaging costs in relation to earnings.

Obviously, packing your product yourself is the cheapest option. When I started I found that cling film was a very acceptable wrap for postcards. Firstly because it is transparent, so that the postcard image could be seen, and formed the front of the pack. Thus the packaging came close to mimicking proper shrink-wrapping and looked attractive whilst at the same time allowing the retailer to see what was in the package. Secondly I could vary the pack size at will, depending on the order. The down-side was that it was time-consuming to do the packaging myself.

Packaging is very dependent on product, though. For instance, cling film might do for postcards, and even books, but it would be useless for posters, where the poster needs good protection from the bumps and scrapes likely to be encountered in the selling environment. Cardboard tubes are far better, especially if they have a mini picture of the poster on the outside.

The alternative to doing it yourself is post-production wrapping by your printer, or by a packaging company. This is more expensive, and to an extent less flexible, especially if you are producing your first self-published product. This is because you will not be in a good position to judge the packet size that your distributors will want to handle. For example, in the postcard market many retailers of art cards want to buy in packs of twelve cards of the same design. But a newsagent will probably be interested in packs of fifty cards of the same design.

So if you have a variety of sales outlets you may need a variety of pack sizes. You would need to order these from a commercial packager before you started selling.

Whichever way you decide to do it, you should aim for packages that are professional in both function and appearance. The package needs to be able to protect your product at every stage of its journey from you to the customer. It is safest to consider it likely that transport and handling damage will occur wherever possible – and pack accordingly.

Packaging to boost sales

Aside from the appearance and function side of packaging I have found it can be used to boost sales to retailers. Early on in my self-publishing career I decided to tell retailers that my postcards came in packs of 50.

This meant that if they wanted to buy at all they bought 50 cards. If I received objections concerning the quantity, I offered to "split a pack" and sold 25. After a time I sold in packs or multiples of 25 as a matter of course. This enabled my packaging to become streamlined and hence more efficient.

I doubt whether I lost any customers through doing this. The only exception I made was for a regular customer who bought a largish number every order, but who liked to change the quantity mix of each card in the range in light of his customers' changing demands and buying preferences.

The other aspect of the packaging mix is point-of-sale wrapping. For instance, most members of the public expect greetings cards to be packaged with envelopes, posters often come with cardboard tubes while books may be shrink-wrapped. Postcards, on the other hand, are usually sold singly and are displayed in racks.

It is possible to boost sales through packaging, though. Suppose you have a range of eight cards, selling as singles. One is not doing so well. One idea is to sell packs of five cards at a discount over the price of five individual cards, always including the slow moving card. Here is an opportunity for selling cards which you might otherwise have to pull from your range, hence the discount may be cost-effective in the long run.

Another idea is to use gift boxes to package different products together. For example, you could bundle together greetings cards, postcards and bookmarks showing local scenes. Doing this can give added value and enable a higher selling price, sufficient to cover the extra cost of the gift packaging.

The general point is that packaging can be use to add perceived value, or help sell otherwise slow moving products.

A classic way to improve profits on posters is to sell them framed, rather than just the poster on its own. You will get far more in extra income because the perceived value is much higher for the framed item. Why? Mainly because you have made an aesthetic choice for the customer, saving them the effort of choosing, not to mention the time and inconvenience of getting the framing done themselves.

Selling skills

A key to selling is confidence in yourself. It is essential to have a positive mental approach to your business, your product and your abilities. If you have a positive approach you will be motivated, and therefore more able to sell. But how to engender the confidence in the first place?

Confidence comes from self-belief in part, and from being successful. If you are self-publishing then you must believe in yourself to start with, otherwise you are going to find life an uphill struggle.

So, you may believe in your basic abilities as a freelance and you have some great imagery to sell. What next?

Well you know what you have to sell, and who to sell it to, so all you need do now is go out and sell it. But if you've never done this before you will probably be nervous. How are you going to cope? What happens if you get rejected on your first attempt?

A way to get over some of the stage fright before your first (and subsequent) sales is to try and imagine how a successful sale would go. Go over what you will say in your mind before the sale, and what you will do if things go badly. But when you get to the retailer don't think of all the things that could go wrong; assume you will get a sale. Take your mind off negative thoughts by humming a tune or thinking of your favourite meal. Say to yourself "you can do it", and don't be afraid of failure, or of the retailer.

Once into the selling situation be pleasant and friendly. Don't let nerves lead you to talk quickly or to be short with your client. Imagine what you would feel like if you were the buyer and the seller was being abrupt, or even rude to you. You would be less inclined to buy, even if you liked the product. So always try to be courteous despite the times when your patience is being stretched to breaking point.

Try not to criticise or find fault with what your buyer says, and do not correct them. Simply confine yourself to being concise about what you are selling and professional in your approach. Do your best to avoid arguing, or discussing or expressing opinions. Your aim is to get on with your potential buyer and make a sale.

You will meet a wide variety of people in your attempts to sell your products. Reacting to them in a professional way, smiling and being pleasant, will help overcome barriers and establish good communication. If your buyer does not like you then your chances of making a sale are limited.

Your dress is a powerful means of influencing the impression you give to others. Therefore you should pay attention to your garb, and the likely effect it will have on your prospective customers. If you turn out looking scruffy or ill-kempt you are likely to get a negative reaction to you and your product. This doesn't mean you have to wear a pinstripe suit when selling, but it does mean looking presentable.

When talking to your buyer make sure you speak clearly and directly to them. Don't sound bored, or uninterested in whether the sale is made or not. But don't talk too fast, or sound so up front and smart that the buyer stops listening to what you are saying and instead starts noticing your sales technique!

Talk with conviction and vivacity. Being articulate and knowledgeable about your product without wasting words will probably get you more sales than a monotonous, lengthy delivery. Be enthusiastic about what you are selling. If you aren't then the buyer is unlikely to show interest. Try to be demonstrative, get good inflection into your voice, look the customer in the eye, and don't slouch or slump in your seat. Act as you would if you were explaining your favourite meal, or piece of music, or film, or moment, to a friend.

In short, hold a conversation with your buyer.

Time and place

When you are asking a buyer to consider the purchase of your product it is better to do it at a time and in a place which provides the best chance of your customer being relaxed and in a receptive mood for buying. This means you too can be fairly relaxed, and if you are you stand a better chance of selling.

Often you will be asked to wait until the buyer is free to deal with you, even if you have made an appointment. It is almost certain if you have not. Learn to take this as part and parcel of selling. If you get impatient you will give out a negative vibe and reduce your chances.

If you are on a tight time schedule and have to leave, then make another appointment for another day. If you are displaying your wares, for example showing off your new postcards, then try to do so when you and the buyer feel comfortable. Don't stand over the customer, and give them plenty of time to consider your product. If possible try to position yourself side-by-side with your potential purchaser; it is more friendly and less confrontational than standing or sitting directly opposite them.

If the buyer is interrupted just as you are getting into your stride, don't let it throw you. Simply wait patiently until you have their attention again. Spend the time thinking about how many cards or posters or whatever you are going to sell. Trying to predict the outcome at these moments is good practice for assessing the likely result of any selling venture.

You can try to move the sale forward by setting the scene for a sale. For example you can start by appealing to the buyer's apprehension that they may be missing a good thing, or that they will make money out of it, or that you are about to sell out. You could also appeal to their sense of pride in having the very latest imagery on sale.

If you have captured the buyer's attention with a lead in, then follow up quickly with your presentation of the product, being as clear and concise as you can.

Showing your samples

Now you have to present your product in its best light.

For example, you should never apologise for the product or point out that things could have been done better. If you do you will only make your customer question why you didn't put the product right before trying to sell it. You will look very unprofessional. So even if you think you could have taken the picture in a slightly better light, don't say so.

If there is a tiny blemish on an item, don't mention it. To you it might be glaringly obvious, but to the buyer, and most likely to the end-user, it is of no consequence. If it is then your buyer will almost certainly see it.

If you are selling a range of products, for example a set of postcards, then it is a good idea to take them all along to the presentation. Showing just one card and then trying to sell the rest will be an uphill struggle. If the remainder of your set is as good as the sample card you have, then showing them will give you a better chance of selling them all. Most buyers, including the general public, like to see what they are paying for.

If necessary, leave samples of your products for the buyer to evaluate at their leisure. If you are trying to sell through the post, or over the telephone, send samples too.

Another important lesson is to listen to what your buyers are telling you. Be interested in what they have to say. Staring out of the window or into space while they are talking will not go down well. And don't interrupt. Remember that speech is silver, but silence is golden. More importantly, by listening you may discover information about your customer which will allow you to tailor your selling to them and increase you chances of selling regularly.

The sales proposal

Once you have set up the selling situation, and gone through the preliminaries, you should be thinking of closing the sale. But there is a big difference between taking an order and selling.

Consider the following selling scenario. You have a range of eight postcards and you are talking to a retailer who is interested in buying.

He or she is looking through them, making comments like "Oh that one's nice, I'll have that one", and "No I don't think that has the right colours; I'll leave that one this time." You end up taking an order for five out of your range of eight cards.

Okay, you can feel pleased to have an order for some of your cards. After all, some is better than none. But you have not done any *selling*. What you have done is simply collected an order, and really it would have been a better use of your time if the retailer had sent the order through the post, based on no more than looking at samples.

So what is it to sell rather than just take an order? Consider the scenario again. Your buyer is thumbing through your cards and says "Oh that's nice"; this is your chance to do some selling by responding with a comment like: "My whole range has sold very well, especially in your kind of shop."

Or: "That card is particularly popular, and other retailers tell me that their customers buy three or four cards from the range at a time. How many packs of each card will suit your turnover?"

You could go even further and suggest that "Your customers will be very pleased to see this range in your shop, especially because they add to the rest of your stock by being different. A big display will be very impressive. Can I suggest you take five packs of each design."

In other words, selling is about enhancing your sales, creating a positive attitude to your product on the part of your buyer, and then closing the sale by making a definite selling proposal to the buyer.

Selling guidelines

So what guidelines could serve to assist in closing sales? Here are six which you could consider in relation to your own selling situation.

First, think of, and use simple key words to sell your product. What you are looking for are words which evoke ready images or emotions. You want to stir the imagination of your buyer. Your aim is to conjure up the wants your customer has and vividly demonstrate how your product matches them.

Second, assume that you are going to make the sale, and that it will be closed. This is a shorthand way of saying act with confidence. Confidence that you will make the sale and confidence that your product is worth the business. Think to yourself that the buyer should purchase your product because it will help *them* gain sales. Do not, however, mistake over-eagerness for confidence. If you are over-eager you could start to pressure the buyer and lose the sale.

Third, during your conversation keep asking straightforward questions which the buyer can only answer yes to. For example you could say "would you like to increase your turnover?", or "do you want your shop to stock the best postcards in the city?", and so on. The aim is to keep a string of yes answers coming so that when you ask for the order the answer is also likely to be yes.

Fourth, ask questions based on the assumption that the sale is closed. These are questions about delivery dates, methods of payment and the like. For example: "Will tomorrow be suitable for delivery?" or "is this order charged to your branch account or to head office?" If you get yes responses to these questions you will know the sale is made. You can go further and try questions like "How do you spell the name of your shop?" or "What is the full address of the shop?" and then write the answer straight on to the invoice or order form. If your buyer gives the appropriate answer you know he or she is buying.

Remember, if your customer has agreed to see you in the first place there was already an initial interest in making a possible purchase. What you are doing is assuming that there is going to be a purchase, and you are acting accordingly.

Fifth, don't forget to actually ask for the order! This is a tense moment because it is at this point that the customer can say no. Don't fall into the temptation to speak fast or to rush the order-taking in order to avoid rejection. If you meet fresh objections from the buyer adopt a problem-solving approach, and look for ways to overcome the objections.

Finally, close the sale at the first possible opportunity. Do not keep talking just for the sake of it, and avoid telling the buyer what a good decision they just made. If your customer tells you what he or she wants as soon as you walk through the door, be grateful. Ditch your sales pitch. Otherwise the buyer will get very impatient with you and you could easily lose a sale from someone who was ready to buy!

Closing the sale

There are several ways to close the sale at this point. The key to them is that you make a selling proposition to the buyer. So, for example, you offer an alternative: "Do you want three or four packs of each design?" Or you suggest a larger order than you think the customer will actually buy and let them respond with a lower order which you then accept. Honour is satisfied on both sides.

You can also simply make a bold proposal like: "I'll write the order out, and I'll need you to sign here." Alternatively you can stop talking and wait in silence, pen poised above the order book. The buyer will feel they need to do something in the silence, and so orders.

Don't be afraid to take your order book out early. If you do you are assuming you will get an order, which is good. Also your buyer will get used to the idea that you want an order. If you get your order book out at the end of your sales presentation you give the buyer the opportunity to reconsider; you have introduced something new at the point of closing the sale.

If you try to close early, but don't succeed, then you will have other opportunities, whereas if you leave the close until the very end of your sales pitch you only have the one chance. Thus try to watch for suitable moments to make a closing offer. Experience will teach you what to look for. It could be something simple like your buyer leaning forward slightly, or displaying a slightly greater interest in something you've said. Whatever it is, it gives you the opportunity to state your sales proposition and close the sale. If you miss the moment then be alert for the next one.

Closing the sale is something that becomes more comfortable with practice, as does selling in general. Practice on your friends, and on buyers who you are fairly sure of. Try closing sales early to see what it feels like. For sure it will feel uncomfortable to start with, but given time you will be able to make selling part of your business. If you don't you will not be maximising your sales potential.

By aiming to close early you save your time and your buyer's; you avoid saying too much and thereby losing a sale; you get several chances to close, not just one; and finally, you appear more businesslike and professional.

Increasing sales

There are several ways of making each sales contact more productive by increased sales.

The first, and perhaps most obvious way, is to close one product sale yet keep your options open on other products in your range. For example, you have just sold your postcards to a buyer and taken the order. Next you get your greetings card range out and sell that too.

One way I have found to increase sales of my products is to offer to produce postcards on commission when I'm selling my standard range. Some of the cards of Manchester University came about like this. So one of my "extra products" is my photographic service which I market at the same time.

However, don't argue with your customer if they don't want the additional service or product. You will only antagonise them and possibly lose the customer. So, even though you know you can give a good deal to the buyer, and one which they would benefit by, do not argue. You cannot win.

However, if your customer is merely raising objections as to why they cannot use them right now, then that is a sales opportunity for you. If you can meet the objection, and get an order – then bingo!

For example, you offer to produce some postcards on commission, but your buyer says no, it is too expensive this month. So you come back with an offer to do it later, with a guarantee that the price will not go up in that time.

A more difficult situation is one where you have a good idea of what quantity your buyer will take, but you want to sell more. Here you could try pointing out what a heavy demand there is for your product. This can work, especially when you are selling a seasonal product. For instance, postcards tend to do well in the summer when demand is swelled by extra tourists. Drawing attention to this is a sensible thing to do.

A lot of insurance selling is based on fear of loss, and the same emotion can be employed to suggest that unless the buyer takes a larger order they might miss the peak in demand and hence not make as much profit as they could. Be careful though, if you use this type of approach, because it puts the buyer under pressure, and pressure selling can be counter-productive.

However there is no point pretending that you are not trying to sell, and if the above situation is genuine then you can use it. The buyer will be able to see the sense in it.

Bulk sales

A third way of increasing sales is the standard method of offering price discounts for bulk purchase. As previously mentioned, here you need to have worked out the discount structure in advance and to have built it in to your costings. Also you need to be acutely aware of the impact of the discount in selling terms.

What you are trying to balance is price versus increased quantity. For example, you normally sell postcards in packs of 25. Your discount should tempt a buyer into a larger purchase that still makes good economic sense for you. So you could offer 10% off a minimum purchase of 250 cards. However, it may never be worth it to the buyer to purchase 250 cards. It could take so long to sell them that they are just hanging around and not selling, or taking up space which could be used for new products.

Therefore offering 10% for 100 cards makes better selling sense. You can then also increase the discount for larger quantities, say 25% for 250 cards. Bear in mind, though, that if your buyer is a regular customer it may be more profitable for you to sell in small quantities at no discount. It is all a question of matching your and the customer's needs and benefits, and you will get a feel for it by trying out different trade-offs.

It is not just a question of increasing the discount either, I once offered 33% on postcards for packs of 250 and still got no sale! Remember, simply selling on price can compromise the perceived benefits your product offers the marketplace.

Negotiation

Up until now I have been talking mainly about the making of a selling proposition in contrast to order taking. However you may get into situations which demand some kind of negotiation. Negotiation is simply where you and your buyer will each be trying to gain a trading advantage by asking for benefits or making concessions.

At first sight this might appear to you to be no more than an attempt to gain the upper hand at your buyer's expense. This is not the way to look at negotiating though. You and your buyer will both have an idea of what each really wants, and of what is less important. It is only where you both think the same thing is equally important that conflict could arise.

For example, if price is crucial then you want the best price for your product, and your buyer wants the cheapest. However as soon as you are prepared to shift on price for, say, a bulk order, or if your buyer is prepared to pay more for same-day delivery, you can negotiate.

Before entering into a negotiating process it is as well to be prepared; to know your ground. A broad appreciation of the trading situation is a good idea. So you should try and decide what may be the comparative strengths and weaknesses, and the needs of both parties, in respect of the transaction at hand. Assess how urgent a conclusion is for yourself and the other side. Then decide how important it is to you to be negotiating. Is it worth your time and effort?

Good negotiation requires preparation, and may not seem worth it for simple selling. But if a long-term business deal is on the cards you might feel it essential to strike the right bargain.

Outlining a negotiating strategy calls for a lot of preparation in terms of gathering information about alternatives and considering the possible effects of not agreeing. Once started, having a sure grasp of your position will make you less vulnerable to intimidating tactics.

In the negotiations you will need to listen to what the other side wants and look for any clues as to what they are prepared to concede on. You can help to uncover the latter by asking questions and probing for positions which may not be firmly held. It is also important to keep the negotiations moving. Making flat objections to proposals won't help this process and may get an emotional reaction which could prove difficult to overcome.

Striking the bargain

So if you are ready to negotiate, the next stage is to list the things you hope to achieve during the course of your bargaining. Also, you should decide your limits: the point beyond you will not go.

For example, in agreeing a business deal involving posters, you may negotiate with a distributor who is going to handle all your poster sales nationwide. You need to decide what percentage payment to the distributor is acceptable to you, what you will agree in terms of losses (of posters) while they are stored at the distributors premises, what you can contribute to advertising costs, over what time scale the payments made to them should reach you, and so on. On all these points you should decide your initial position, and the threshold below which the terms become unacceptable.

You may think you need the distributor more than they need you, but don't forget they will probably be in competition too, and business is business. Only where there is no overlap between the maximum you are prepared to offer, and the minimum the other side is prepared to accept, is no negotiation possible. Of course the art of negotiation is in discovering where the limits lie.

In the end you are going to have to trade concessions. Knowing what these are, and using the concession to maximum effect, will be easier with good preparation. If you need time to think about a proposal don't be afraid to do so. A cool nerve and a steady hand are useful attributes. Try not to give away concessions unless you get something in return. Always keep your eye on your main objectives, whatever the other side is doing.

And at the end of a negotiation it is very sensible to summarise what has been agreed, so there is no room for misunderstanding.

Cultivate your selling skills

At the end of the day, selling is a crucial part of a successful business. If you are in self-publishing for commercial reasons there is no way you can avoid it. Its basis is good marketing, but the rest, as they say, is down to you – your presentation and selling skills.

If you find this prospect daunting, don't worry. You may think your only ability lies in producing good imagery. But if you believe in yourself, and your product, you can learn selling, and practice becoming better at it. After all, nothing ventured, nothing gained.

If something works, do more of it, and try to uncover the formula for success. Don't give up. You will be bound to get some rejections, but taking them in your stride is a part of business life. Always try to keep a way to sell open, and present buyers with related options if you can.

Finally, good selling depends on being well organised, both in terms of time and in knowing who will buy and with what regularity. Therefore keep accurate sales records, and put serious effort into getting new buyers.

CHAPTER CHECKLIST

- Have you thought through your marketing before selling your products?
- Are you selling direct to customers or using a distribution network?
- Have you set selling targets?
- Have you decided on your selling method? Is it face-to-face selling, telephone selling, selling through advertising, or a combination of these?
- Do you believe in your product?
- Do you have a positive attitude to the product and the sale?
- Have you got a clear idea of what benefits you offer, and who they suit?
- Have you formed an opinion of your customers?
- Have you considered the best selling approach for the customers you have identified?
- Have you decided what price to put on the perceived value of your product?
- Have you decided on a suggested retail price?
- Have you costed and decided on a discount structure?
- Is your product and the packaging you use attractive?
- Have you arranged for suitable packaging for delivery to the distributor and/or customer?
- Will your delivery packaging promote your professional business image and engender a positive attitude from your distributors?
- Does your packaging add perceived value for the end-user?
- Do you have confidence in yourself?
- Have you gone over what you will say in your mind before the sale?
- Have you assumed you will get a sale?
- Is your approach pleasant and friendly?
- Do you look presentable when selling?
- Have you made sure you are speaking clearly and directly to your clients?
- Have you presented your product in its best light?
- Do you listen to what your buyers are telling you they want?
- Are you closing sales by making a definite selling proposal to the buyer?
- Are you remembering to ask for the order?
- Do you summarise what has been agreed at the end of your negotiations?
- Are you organised in assessing your results?

6 Art Publishing

Until now I have concentrated on self-publishing ventures using commercially based reproduction processes. However it is not necessary to use only these to become a self-publisher. You can still make, market and sell other image-based "publications", for example photographic prints, in much the same way as cards, posters or books.

These alternatives have to be quite different from commercially reproduced publications though. They are destined for different markets, with different values.

The use of processes other than commercial printing inevitably means it is only possible to achieve a small-scale production of images. So it is not only possible, but indeed desirable, to present your imagery as "art" with each item forming an "object" in itself. These can then sell into the art market as individual works of much higher value than mass-produced products.

The art object

The most obvious of these alternatives is photographic prints, either colour or black and white. A fine quality photographic print is a beautiful object in its own right, and hence has a very different kind of value to a postcard, say.

A number of other processes can be used to print on to all sorts of surfaces, not just photographic paper. For example you can use the gum bichromate process to coat high quality drawing paper. Or you can use Polaroid film to deposit an image onto metal, sacking, or some other surface. Another option is to use liquid light-sensitive emulsion to coat any surface you choose, and print directly on to that.

The point of using any of the above processes is that you end up with an "art object" to sell to the public. The way you are publishing the images is not as bulk-produced postcards or posters, but as individually hand-crafted works. Because of this your image is part of something that must be perceived as a work of art, and its price will reflect the value the public is prepared to attach to art objects of that kind.

The different values and means of selling into this market are discussed below, but one important consequence of this approach is that the sale of art-oriented imagery is much more dependent on self-promotion and establishing a "name". Techniques for self-promotion are covered later in the chapter.

Photographic prints

When you produce a photographic print for sale, it pays to find ways to increase its perceived value. There are four ways you can do this.

Firstly, and perhaps most importantly, the print has to be produced to a very high standard consistent with the effect you are trying to achieve. Your aim is to invest the image with that "something extra". If it looks like a snapshot that anyone could have taken with any old camera then you are going to have an uphill struggle selling it as a unique and precious object.

Among a discerning buying public your print needs to stand out from the standard seen in photographic books, or on posters and the like. Luckily it is possible to print on to photographic paper so that you do get better tonality and range of tones than possible in commercial printing, there being no origination and half-tone process to go through. But it does mean your printing technique has to be up to the mark.

Of course you do not have to do the printing yourself, as long as your printer is good and you can instruct him or her to produce exactly what you want. But to some this may seem like heresy; surely you should be crafting your own prints?

I really don't think it matters from the point of view of the print produced. After all most self-publishers are quite happy with the idea of commercial printing being done by someone else, so why not photographic printing?

However, values do come into it. Because your photographic prints are going to be sold as art objects your buying public may not perceive a print by someone else – even though it is your image – as of such worthwhile value. This view probably varies with the buyer, however. In the end it comes down to what you feel happiest producing.

The debate about this kind of printing issue will certainly continue. Even the most famous photographers tend to split into two camps, those that print their own work, and those that don't. It is an issue that usually doesn't trouble other artists in the same way because they don't have the opportunity to have someone else produce the finished object. Jeff Koons is a notable exception.

Further enhancement

Once you have your fine photographic print you can frame it, using a high quality moulding and doing it in a professional way. It is worth learning how to frame well yourself, because having it done commercially can be expensive.

It is important to think of the frame as part of the finished product because you will be selling it as well. Not only do frames add aesthetic factors to your print, they are also seen as making the whole package worth more. Hence you already have added value and can charge more. To do this successfully though, the frame should obviously be sympathetic to your print and not clash with it. You will have a big variety of mouldings to choose from.

Careful consideration should also be given to the mount. Is the print to be mounted full frame, or masked? If it is masked, the size of the border and its colour need to harmonise with both your print and the frame.

Your next option is to produce a stated limited run of the print. Many people think it is easy to print up a photograph; after all if they can't do it themselves they can always pop down to the local minilab for a set of prints. In other words the perceived value of a standard photographic print is generally low in the public's mind, and so they are not prepared to pay a lot for it. But if you can produce a stunning print in limited quantities then you increase the perceived value.

So producing only 25 prints of the same image will give the print rarity value. Producing 250 prints will lessen the effect, but is still better than your print being any old photograph.

Finally you can sign your print, next to the print number. It is usual to put the date on too, but it is up to you. The fact that your signature is there gives the print a little extra kudos, especially if you are becoming well known.

When you are producing an art object you are to some extent selling your name as well as the object. You are making a personal statement. If you feel all this is rather pretentious, remember that you are actually selling in the art world, where the values are different to commercial photography. Also bear in mind that you would happily put your name on to your commercially produced poster or postcard, even if it is just next to the copyright sign.

It is often easier to make distinctive art-based imagery if you use non-standard processes, some of which were touched upon above. These, if used well, will produce "objects" which have a high perceived value, partly because the buying public will not know how you've done it, and because using the processes almost inevitably means you will have had to produce the work yourself in limited quantities.

It is not the purpose of this book to cover such processes in detail; for those who are interested such information can be found elsewhere (see "Further Reading" at the back of this book). But just to give you an idea of the range of possibilities, below I will briefly outline four processes, three photographic and one an alternative printing method.

Non-silver processes

First you can use one of the older, non-silver, ways of making light sensitive materials. These include cyanotypes and gum bichromate. The gum bichromate process uses contact printing. You can choose your own paper or cloth as a base. The final image ends up consisting of water-colour or gouache in any colour you choose.

To make up a paper-based print choose a good quality drawing paper. Soak the paper, tape it to a board, and let it dry so it stretches. Then coat the paper, using cotton wool or a roller, with a mixture of gum arabic, potassium dichromate and a water-based colour pigment. The potassium dichromate hardens the gum when exposed to light, particularly ultra-violet light. However the light sensitivity is very low so the process takes some time.

Contact print your negative, then soak the print in water. This washes away the unhardened areas of gum, leaving just the picture. Leave to dry.

Make sure you wear rubber gloves for this process as the chemicals involved are toxic and can be absorbed by the skin.

The finished product looks very like a fine art print. It is feasible to run the same print through the process several times to gain contrast and depth and it is possible to add further water-colour paint to selected areas if desired. Different colours can be used in the subsequent printings. Experimenting with the process should give you an idea of what it is possible to achieve.

A way of using a variety of base materials like metal, canvas, wood or ceramics, as well as paper, is to use liquid emulsion and paint or spray it on to your chosen surface. You can mix your own chemicals or buy ready to use ones. The emulsions are sensitive to light in the way photographic paper is, so use safe lighting and an enlarger to expose the negative on to your chosen surface. This gives you the advantage of not only using contact printing. If the surface you are coating is highly absorbent, like plaster for instance, then sizing it first will save on emulsion.

Process the emulsion in regular print developer and fixer.

Image transfer

Another way to create distinctive art imagery is to make use of Polaroid material and try the image transfer technique. What you need for this is a camera capable of taking a Polaroid back, so medium and large format users will be able to take advantage of this if they already have a back. Others can try out the process too if they can get hold of a slide printer which takes a Polaroid film back. Also required is some Polaroid "peel apart" film.

Polaroid film, when used normally, is exposed and then pulled through rollers which burst pods of chemicals which then develop the film. After a fixed amount of time the print is developed, and is peeled away from the rest of the material. When using the image transfer technique, instead of waiting the recommended time for print development you peel apart after a short time – around ten seconds. The print part is discarded, and the "negative" part is placed wet side down on to a surface – paper or anything else you like – that will take the image. Watercolour paper is a good medium.

You then apply pressure, using a roller for example. The image that would have been reproduced on to the print part of the Polaroid is now transferred to your chosen surface.

The technique works best with images which don't rely on detail for their impact.

If you use a wet paper surface to take the image the effect is to diffuse the image compared to using the paper dry. Again, trying the process out with a variety of changes in the way it is done will show what is possible.

Silk screen printing

Finally I will mention a non-photographic process which can use photographs as a base from which to produce fine art prints. This is silk screen printing.

In this process the image is produced using a stencil, which is supported on a screen. The screen used to be made of silk, hence the name of the process, but is more commonly made of a synthetic fibre today. The screen is stretched over a frame of wood or metal, and ink is spread over the screen by a rubber squeegee. This squeezes the ink through the screen and on to the printing surface. The stencil holds back the ink in non-image areas.

You can make the stencil either by hand or photographically. Hand stencils are not very practical for printing images, so a photo stencil is best for this. These can be prepared either directly or indirectly. In the direct method a light sensitive solution is applied straight on to the screen, then contacted with the image and exposed to light. The image areas of the coating, which are unhardened by light, are then washed away with chemicals.

In the indirect method a stencil film is used. A positive is produced using four-colour or halftone origination, and this is contacted with the stencil film and exposed to light. The stencil is then transferred to the screen and the backing film removed, leaving the mesh blocked in the non-image areas.

Silk screen presses are often manually operated, and these are very cheap. They are therefore well suited to handmade prints with an artistic edge to them. However it is possible to get semi-automatic and fully automatic presses capable of producing up to 6000 impressions per hour. This technique is an ideal process for posters. In addition the screen can be used to print colour on to a variety of surfaces like metal or plastic.

Self-promotion

It should be clear by now that using such art-based printing processes is rather different from the more broadly commercial ones discussed earlier in the book. The different processes mean a different scale of production is achieved, and in consequence a different attitude and presentation is often needed.

Small scale printing means taking extra care in the artistic "feel" of your product. You will be putting more of "the artist" into your output than if you self-publish using the commercial processes. So as an artist or craft worker you may feel this makes you less of a business person. However all the principles of marketing apply equally well to this kind of product as they do to the commercially-based products.

Also, the advice on selling is just as relevant. However there is a distinction, and that is that your "art" is more likely to sell in a different type of venue, such as galleries, rather than in retail outlets. In addition your "name" as an artist becomes more important in the setting of your prices, and hence your financial success. Therefore self-promotion should be given serious consideration.

There are several ways to get your name, and your work, better known. The most obvious is to get into the local, and even national, newspapers, as having produced some outstanding work of art.

Publicity through newspapers

At the local level this is not as difficult as you may think. Local newspapers are always on the lookout for interesting items with a local connection for their features pages. If you have produced some work showing local places, then prepare a press release saying what you have done. Include some information about yourself too. For example, include your age and previous experience, especially if it is relevant to local institutions. Explain why you have produced this work and what it means to you.

An alternative is to simply ring the newspaper and ask to speak to the features editor. Have an idea of what you are going to say when you do this. Try to script the conversation beforehand so you don't forget to mention all the relevant points. Features editors will be interested to hear from you, especially if you can tie in your approach with some local event.

If you are having an exhibition locally this can serve as the basis for a feature. Perhaps you are a judge at a local art fair, or as happened to me, my postcards were used as the professional standard in an exhibition of competition entries to find new postcard images for Manchester. An angle like that is always welcomed by the papers.

The key is to make what you are doing interesting to the editor, and persuade him or her that it is of interest to the paper's readers too. Quite often if you are producing novel images – as is likely to be the case using the processes discussed earlier in the chapter – you will find a high degree of interest in what you are doing.

Exhibitions

A great way of getting interest is to hold an exhibition of your work. This means getting the owner or manager of an exhibition space interested in the work and willing to devote his or her time and energy to mounting an exhibition of it. Many galleries are happy to show local talent if it is shown to them. Other, less commercial, venues may include libraries or other public buildings, local institutes, theatre foyers, etc.

A personal appointment to show your work is an essential part of the process. When you meet, the gallery owner or exhibition organiser will be assessing your work to determine whether he or she will take it on. Also, though, you are being appraised as a potential exhibitor. Your approach will matter. Your personality, business manner and attention to all aspects of your work are all important in influencing their decision.

At the same time, however, you should also be weighing up the exhibition space and those involved with it. It is not all one way traffic, despite the fact that you will be keen to get your work shown and sold. You should try to determine how knowledgeable they are about art, and about photography-based work in particular. Are you dealing with an enthusiastic promoter of the arts, or someone just doing the job for want of some other alternative? Determine whether your work is going to get a fair promotion or is just filling in space.

Being offered an exhibition is an exciting moment, especially if you are given a solo exhibition. The latter will mean a significant body of your output being on show with the chance for you to make a big impact, as each of your works can reinforce the others, rather like a range of postcards.

Simply exhibiting in a gallery or public space is a boost to the ego, helps promote your name and adds to your artistic credentials, but it doesn't help the money roll in. What helps your business as a self-publisher – whatever vehicle you are using for your imagery – is sales.

Most artists sell much of their work through gallery-held exhibitions, and you should be no exception. Of course a gallery will want a commission for selling your work, which is fair enough since this covers the gallery overheads and so on.

So your approach to a gallery is not simply about showing your work to a wider audience, but about selling your product. You must decide whether you like the style of the gallery and what you think their attitude to selling is. Thus a businesslike attitude is also necessary.

Gallery sales

If a gallery likes your work and you can agree, then you may be offered a choice of arrangement – consignment selling, an exhibition, or an offer of gallery representation. It is usual for sales of work at an exhibition to be on a consignment basis. But it is a good idea to have a written agreement which includes more than just the selling details.

Consignment selling is essentially an agreement for you to leave your work at the gallery, which undertakes to sell it for you. The gallery gives you the proceeds of the sale less an agreed commission. Most galleries will work on a sale or return basis, so will keep your work for a fixed period before sending it back to you if it remains unsold.

There are several less positive sides to sale or return. First you have to wait to be paid, which affects your cash flow. Second the gallery has little incentive to actively promote and sell your goods. They have no capital tied up in them – although they do of course need to pay their overheads and make a profit too – and work that is not selling is taking up space which could house other more saleable goods. Third, you will have to take your stock back if it is unsold. If your work is topical or seasonal this can leave you with dead stock on your hands.

You may like to counter these disadvantages by agreeing a formal contract between yourself and the gallery owner. Then you will know where you stand. If you are on a sale or return basis you can negotiate the retail price the gallery sells at. You can agree the commission rate, arrange that the gallery covers the insurance whilst your work is in their hands, and finally you can reach a mutually acceptable period of notice for either side to terminate the agreement should your work not be selling.

Most important of all is to make sure your agreement is in writing, and identifies the work you are consigning to the gallery. If you don't do this, sorting out an insurance claim in the event your work is stolen from the gallery, or damaged by fire, will be a real headache. To this end make sure the work itself can be identified as yours. Sign it, tag it or otherwise mark it.

Your agreement should also have a clause dealing with the situation where your work has been damaged while on display at the gallery. Failure to agree this in advance could lead to some acrimonious exchanges, which won't help your future business dealings.

Once you have consigned work make sure you keep accurate records of where it is, and when it is sold or returned.

In general an exhibition agreement should incorporate the following factors: an identification of the works to be exhibited, their description and price; the duration of the exhibition; the publicity and who is responsible for it, including its cost; provision of promotional material by you, for example biographical detail; the packaging and transport arrangements; the transit insurance and the insurance of your work while at the exhibition; the security and safety arrangements at the exhibition venue; the framing and hanging of your work; the exhibition preview time, date, and who is responsible for its cost; the conditions of sale, whether a deposit is required, and whether any works are not for sale; the commission on sales; payment arrangements to you; arrangements for any unsold work; whether you are restricted in exhibiting elsewhere during the exhibition.

Also, of course, you need to establish the names and addresses of all parties to the agreement and have their signatures and the date appended to it.

Finally you might be offered gallery representation, especially following a successful exhibition. Essentially this is an offer by the gallery to act as a manager or agent for you. The gallery will undertake to promote, exhibit and sell your work.

When you accept such an offer you will be capitalising on that gallery's reputation. Your name will then be associated with the gallery and with other artists who are also represented by them. All this is of benefit to you provided the reputation of the gallery is a good one, it reaches a wide audience, and the other artists' work enhances yours rather than the other way round – your work could even be dragged down by others.

If you become part of a gallery roster in this way it is likely the gallery may insist that any work you sell, whether exhibited in the gallery or not, should attract a commission. Again you need to be fully aware of the terms under which the gallery is representing you. At least establish the nature of the agency, its extent, the duration of the agreement and how it may be terminated, selling prices, insurance, commission, payment arrangements, and arrangements for the return of work to you.

Craft fairs and shows

If exhibitions are the glamorous end of selling art-based objects, then craft fairs and shows involve you in the nitty-gritty of selling direct to the public against competition from other art and craft workers. They will be selling things different to yours, with a differing price structure and with different ways of displaying and selling. Nonetheless you are all after the same money – that of the people attracted to the show by the promise of crafts for sale.

The nature of these shows really puts your promotional and sales technique into the spotlight. This is so because of how this sort of show works. It is set up in a venue for a day, or a weekend, with people coming in without any fixed notion of what they are going to buy, but probably wanting to spend something on a piece of craft. The question is, what are they going to spend it on?

First of all they will be looking for something that attracts their eye. This is where your ability to mount a good display and promote a good product are brought to bear. You will be attending your stall, but you should also be willing to talk to people about your craft and the products you have made. Some people are keen to know something of the technicalities of it. After all, they are not buying an anonymous piece, but are purchasing it direct from the artist. Thus you are not just selling the work, but also an additional intangible benefit.

You can also use your conversation to get direct feedback from the buying public on their likes and dislikes, and possibly even secure a commission to make something specially for them. If you do, ensure that you have a written order which specifies what you will produce for them, its price, and the delivery date.

It pays, therefore, to tell your customers something about the product, how it was made, and something about yourself – the reason you made the work and your artistic intentions.

During the show you will need to make sure your stall is attended at all times. However, you can also find time to chat to other stall-holders and pick up valuable advice and marketing information.

Once the show has finished you will need to process all the orders you have taken for further work, and list all the contacts you have made and any new customers. Building up a customer list may mean you can sell direct to them in the future, simply by mailing them a catalogue of your production.

Then you should assess whether the show was worthwhile for you. Did your sales and orders justify the outlay for the stall, the cost of transport and your time? Judge the venue against others you may have been to, and in light of what you have learned from other traders at the show.

CHAPTER CHECKLIST

● Are you interested in small-scale production of imagery?
● Are you able to produce "art" based products?
● Have you considered alternative methods for producing imagery?
● How can your product be presented and sold as a valuable object?
● Remember that framing, limiting the run and signing the work add value.
● Your name as an artist helps to sell work, and thus is important to your prices and your financial success.
● Have you given self-promotion serious consideration?
● Have you considered holding an exhibition?
● Consider your personality, business manner and all aspects of your work in relation to a gallery and its owner.
● Have you weighed up the gallery as suitable to meet your needs as an artist?
● Have you considered craft fairs as a sales outlet?

7 Business Matters

In this chapter I am going to cover a range of issues connected with running a business as a self-publisher. Many individuals think of tax and other business matters as the most unexciting part of being creative and entrepreneurial. Dry they can be, but they are central to your success and future growth. It will pay to get to grips with them right at the start of your self-publishing venture.

It is at this point that you should re-examine your motives. If you are self-publishing as a hobby-based activity then making a profit and future business expansion probably doesn't concern you. But if your interest is any greater than this then, dry or not, you need to get to grips with business and financial issues.

You cannot make a profit unless you are organised properly, know what you are selling each month, and what your costs are. Still less can you plan for the future without knowing what the present holds. Even if you are an out-and-out hobbyist you will benefit from sound business organisation, especially when it comes to filling in your tax return.

To help with this and running a business efficiently, this chapter will discuss business type, business organisation, financial matters, tax and other legalities.

Sole trading

An early decision to make is what kind of business structure you are going to adopt. For the self-publisher the choice will often come down to being fully self-employed, or freelancing whilst holding down another job. Other options are setting up a partnership or a limited company. The rules and regulations governing these types of business structure can change from time to time, so you should check the current state of affairs before entering into any one of them. What follows should be taken as a guide only.

If you are self-employed and operating alone, then this means being your own boss and making the business decisions. It also means being taxed as a self-employed person.

The Inland Revenue poses several questions to help you determine whether you are self-employed, and these are instructive. A "yes" answer to any of them puts you in the self-employed category. Among the questions are the following: Do you have the final say in how the business is run? Are you risking your own money in the business? Do you have the responsibility for the losses as well as the profits? Do you provide the major pieces of equipment you need to do your job? Do you have to correct unsatisfactory work in your own time and at your own expense?

Most freelances will answer yes to some of these questions, at least in connection with their self-publishing ventures. Thus they are self-employed, and if they are on their own they are operating as sole traders in a business sense. Holding down another job at the same time as an employee does not affect that status, as each job is assessed separately.

As a sole trader you will be liable for business losses, to the extent of all your assets and possessions. Think about this before you borrow large sums of money to finance your self-publishing activities.

Partnerships and companies

If you are thinking of a publishing venture in association with someone else then you could form a partnership. This is very attractive to some people because it provides an opportunity to share the work and spread the risk. In addition you have someone else to talk to about the project, which makes it more sociable and can generate ideas.

However, it also means that your control over the business can be less direct. For instance, if your partner decides to buy something like a new piece of equipment, you are bound by the decision once carried out. Or if your partner lets down a major buyer, you will be liable as well. Indeed, any contract made by a partner on behalf of the business will bind the other partners legally.

Every partner is liable for the business's losses, almost to the full extent of all assets and possessions. Partners are liable both "jointly" (as a partnership) and "severally" (as individuals). The latter means that if your partner can't meet his or her liabilities, you must.

Partnerships can be set up by a deed that can include the purpose of the business, the authority to enter into contracts on behalf of the partnership, procedures for resolving partnership disputes, the rights to profits, and the procedures to be followed for dissolving the partnership.

Another business structure which could eventually appeal to the self-publisher, especially if getting involved in large-scale publishing, is the limited company.

Setting up a limited company creates a legal entity separate from you personally. The effect, usually, is to limit the liability to the company's assets, and not your personal ones. There is a legal procedure to follow in setting up a limited company, which will result in the company being registered.

Seek advice from your solicitor, bank manager and accountant about the advantages and disadvantages, and the necessary conditions involved.

The business plan

Once you have decided on a business structure it is a good idea to prepare a business plan. If you are starting up as a sole trader with your own savings as capital, you may feel this is a waste of valuable time. I would counsel the reverse. Although you may have the basic business idea firm in your mind it makes your ideas explicit if you reproduce them on paper. Doing this will make you aware of just what you are trying to do, and whether it is feasible in the cold light of the written word.

Planning is central to good business practice. It forces you to think ahead and encourages you to be realistic rather than too optimistic.

A business plan is a written account of what you hope to achieve in business and how you intend to achieve it. It helps you to set objectives which you can meet through managing your available resources, your artistic ability, and your capital. The plan also makes it easier to assess how you are doing, by giving you a yardstick against which you can measure your progress.

You can split the plan into several different sections to suit your particular enterprise. Normally you would want to include an introduction which summarises the whole plan at a glance. It can be difficult to get abstract ideas into a summary, so work at it. The discipline encourages a businesslike approach.

The main part of the plan is the business concept based on your analysis of the market and how you aim to meet it in the coming year. From this you should be able to forecast sales, and hence work out your projected cash flow. You should also include an assessment of the business risks you face and how you can deal with them. Thereafter you can work out the likely financing you require, and what your likely profits will be.

Finally, writing down an action plan of how you are going to achieve your business objectives will force you to consider the steps needed for success.

Getting organised

At the risk of stating the obvious, the best kind of business organisation is one which is efficient. In practice that means you can lay your hands on any relevant bit of information when needed. Therefore your filing and information retrieval system should be up to scratch, and what records you keep should cover all eventualities. You yourself will generate plenty of business paperwork, such as statements, invoices and reminders.

There are two main ways to keep business records: on paper and on computer. It doesn't matter which of these you choose as long as your system does the job. The key here is understanding what that job is, and this aspect is dealt with under financial matters later in this chapter.

A basic system which you know backwards is obviously better than a casual approach where you just dump everything to do with the business into a drawer to be sorted out later – doing things that way means you will have no idea of where you stand on a weekly or monthly basis. It will also ensure that you spend lots of time picking through your records before you can start to discover what profit or loss you may have made.

It is a simple matter to set up a file for keeping all business related expenses and income, plus an invoice book for recording sales. Another file should take care of business correspondence, and finally a box file can house cheque stubs and the like.

You have the choice of running your business from home or setting up an office or studio elsewhere. Obviously the choice will be influenced by how much money you earn from your self-publishing business, and whether you are a full time freelance or have another job.

If you are just starting out you will probably work from home. There are several advantages, and some disadvantages, to this. You save money on rent, heat, light and commuting, and reduce the stress of getting to work. You can also set some of the costs against tax. On the other hand it can be a distraction to have your office at home if you have a family or partner at home at the same time. You might find it tempting to always be at work, and thus in conflict with domestic life.

Putting your home address on stationery could also create a non-businesslike image, as could having members of your family answering business telephone calls if you are not available. A telephone answering machine and/or a fax could get round the latter problem.

If you don't already own a personal computer, then you need to consider whether it is worth getting one. If your turnover is small you won't really need one to run the business, but there are several advantages to computerising your office, and the outlay is falling all the time.

Computers

Using a computer will save you time and energy in the long run and provide you with almost instant access to sales figures, expenses and income. In addition, if you have a good quality printer you can also produce business letters and stationery to a high standard.

Using the computer as a word processor will allow you to set up standard letters and letterheads which are very time consuming to produce otherwise. Modern ink jet printers also print envelopes, so making typewriters redundant. You can also use the computer to keep records and caption information for your photographic files, and thus be able to tell quickly what you have in them.

There is a choice between two systems. An Apple Macintosh based one, or a PC (personal computer).

The Apple Mac was the first to make popular a user-friendly interface which didn't require learning an operating system command language. All that was needed was a mouse to control the pointer, or cursor, on the computer screen. The screen produces a representation of a desktop with pictures (or icons as they are referred to in computer-speak) denoting folder or files where you store things, and applications which enable you to do things like word processing.

All that is needed to move things around on the desktop is for you to point to the file using the mouse, and click on it. Once you have done this you can drag the file to another location, or to the "wastebasket" if you want to throw it away. No special language is needed.

Whether you are doing word processing for letters, or using a business spreadsheet to record figures, menus and dialogue boxes give you options for entering and changing things. It is a very simple system to use.

The more recent, alternative system, based on the PC, uses a version of the above called "Windows" which is produced by Microsoft Corporation. As far as the average user (i.e. you and me) is concerned, these two "WIMPS" interfaces do much the same job. There are slight differences, but these are overwhelmed by the similarities.

Your choice will probably come down to a combination of price, function and whether you prefer the visuals of one system over the other. Both computer types will do the job of handling a self-publishing and freelance business for you. And it is possible that the computers of the future will handle both types of interface.

Before you buy, however, make sure you understand what you need the computer to do, and that the model you are considering, and the applications you intend to run on it, really fit the bill.

Undoubtedly the organisation of your business will become more efficient, and your business stationery, invoices, statements, letters and so on will appear very professional, if you computerise. Everything can be given a uniform image which looks very impressive and inspires confidence.

To get top quality output a good printer is essential. Dot matrix printers are the cheapest, but the least good pound for pound. These are now being superseded by ink-jet technology at a reasonable cost. The print quality is high, and the range of typefaces available far greater than before. The latter gives you a wide choice in design for your letter-heads and so on. Thus you can convey a very professional image to your customers.

The best quality comes from laser printers, or those using daisy-wheels, which actually imprint a letter onto the paper like typewriters do. These printers tend to be rather expensive though, and as ink-jet documents do not suffer that much in comparison it makes them very cost effective for the self-publisher.

Again, get a good demonstration of the various options before you buy. It is worthwhile making sure you get a printer which will take envelopes and single sheets of paper, as you will almost certainly want these facilities in running your business.

Financial records

There are several records necessary to ensure that adequate financial information is available. Basically what you want is a record keeping system which helps you control the business side of your activities. For the self-publisher this means not only the usual financial accounts, but also stock records, cash flow forecasts, sales forecasts and new product plans.

The latter four will help with the financial side, but also have the advantage of providing information that will aid in planning for the introduction of future products, or the reordering of old ones. There is often a considerable time lag between ordering a new product or reordering an existing one, and its arrival.

Your accounting system should record receipts and payments, define the assets and liabilities of the business in financial terms, and show the profit or loss you are making. At the end of each accounting period you will have to produce figures for the Inland Revenue so that your tax liability can be assessed.

You will need to keep all invoices and receipts for goods and services paid for, and a copy of all invoices sent to customers. In addition keep bank statements, plus paying-in and cheque-book stubs. Use box files or envelopes for this. If business warrants it you could get a filing cabinet to do the job; you could then store your picture files in it as well.

It is a good practice to update your payments and receipts records daily. Leaving it for longer, say monthly, will mean it will take more time and increase the likelihood of leaving something out.

Pay particular attention to the way you file records. A filing system is only as good as its ability to allow ready retrieval of relevant information. You could file by week, or by function – expenses and receipts for example. Better still you could combine time with function. You will need time-based accounting anyway, because you need to draw up figures for tax purposes which will require it.

Computer-based records allow a considerable amount of cross-referencing for information retrieval purposes, and could replace manual recording using a cash book. You still need to keep all your paper statements and invoices though, in case the Inland Revenue want to see them.

Recording expenses

You also need to keep a record of all expenses that are claimable against tax. Allowable expenses are not always easy to determine, and it is wise, therefore, to check with the Revenue about what is allowable at any given time.

Often you may get asked to claim for what you think is relevant, rather than getting a list from them. This puts you in the position of entering a claim without knowing exactly what will be acceptable. It is more sensible to include as much as possible that appears relevant.

Allowable expenses can include the following: materials such as film and processing; travelling connected with the business, for example fares and hotels; car expenses such as petrol, oil, licence, insurance, repairs and parking; postage and stationery; telephone expenses; depreciation on equipment; repairs to equipment; subscriptions to relevant magazines and professional societies; book purchases relevant to conducting your business; accountant's fees; exhibitions and catalogues; advertising; model fees; capital allowances on equipment costs.

Not all of these can be set against tax at full cost. You, or your accountant, need to work out the percentage basis before you claim. However you should simply record the full expense as you incur it, and sort the tax deductible part out at the end of the tax year.

Petty Cash

For some items it is inconvenient to pay by cheque or credit card and so no record will be available, but minor payments in cash can be made if you set up a petty cash system.

To do this you draw a cheque for a small amount, say £50, and put the money in a container in your office. When you want to buy a small item for the business, or you want to reimburse yourself for a previous cash purchase, you record the nature of the expense, the date, and the amount, on a petty cash docket. You then take the money out of the petty cash container and replace it with the docket. The amount of cash and the dockets will, if the system is running correctly, add up to the original amount drawn out by cheque.

When you run low or out of cash in the container, then draw another cheque bringing the amount of cash back up to the original advance of £50. Then write the amount of the replacement cheque against the items that the petty cash was spent on. In this way they are recorded as a business expense.

Cash flow

The records I have talked about so far can be used to provide a snapshot of business activity at any one time in the past. But it is also useful to try and estimate what will happen in the future, so that you can plan ahead and take a reasonably accurate view of whether or when you can fund new product development, for example.

One way of doing this is to calculate your cash flow over a period. Essentially what you are trying to do is forecast your sales and costs, month by month, in order to get some idea of the amounts you expect to spend and receive, and hence the degree of profit or loss you anticipate. Obviously it is difficult to do this with complete accuracy, but if you can't do it, no-one else can.

If you are borrowing money (discussed below) to finance future production, you will almost certainly have to show forecasts to your lender. You are not going to engender much confidence in the bank manager if all you can do is shrug your shoulders!

When preparing your cash flow budget try to get as close as possible to an accurate forecast. This won't be easy at first, but as you build up business experience you will get a guide from looking back over the first few months activity. You should forecast, month by month, all outgoings on expenses like heat, light, film, processing, stationery, postage, etc., plus all money paid out to suppliers of materials etc. If you are paying yourself out of the business then list that too. This will give you a total monthly figure for outgoings.

Then you should predict all sales and commissions that you receive during the month and convert them into monies coming in to the business. Next you can work out the profit or loss each month, and finally produce a running total for each month over the whole year. When you have done this you can tell at a glance when you might be short of money and when you might have a surplus.

If you have borrowed money to start the business, then the interest and repayments on the loan should be included in your cash flow calculations.

Throughout the year you can enter the actual cash flow next to your forecast. If they look very different it will alert you to look for the reason. It could be you simply got your initial forecasts wrong through lack of experience, but it might be that things are not going as well as expected. If you know this early you can take steps to sort out any problems as they arise, rather than wait until your accounting year ends.

Borrowing money

You will need money for starting your self-publishing business (seed capital), running it (working capital), and for expanding or replacing your product line.

You can raise the necessary finance through several different routes, in combination or otherwise. First, of course, you need to work out what will be required for each phase of the business cycle, but obviously if you are just starting out the start-up and running costs will concern you most. You can get an appreciation of these two elements by including the initial finance in your cash flow calculations.

Once you have estimated your capital needs there are two main ways to meet them: equity capital or debt finance. Equity capital is money supplied by you as the owner of the business and will probably come out of your savings. It is, therefore, the amount the business owes you. If you are setting the business up as a partnership, then your partners could also contribute equity capital on an agreed basis. To raise additional equity capital you could sell part of your business, with the contributors having a share in the after-tax profits.

The alternative way to raise money is to go into debt. Some will find this prospect abhorrent, but there are certain advantages. First, you do not have to surrender to others a share of your equity or control of your business. Second, the interest you pay to service the debt is tax deductible. Third, you can repay the debt when it suits your business interests, and when you have the necessary finance. In other words you have a degree of control and flexibility.

There are, however two main disadvantages. First, the debt must be paid off eventually, within the terms of the loan, whereas equity can be retained in the business for its lifetime. Second, the interest payments must be made irrespective of whether the business is making a profit or not. Failure to pay off the loan or meet the interest payments could result in bankruptcy.

Clearly you need to ensure that the returns on your debt finance are greater than the net after-tax interest rates on the loan. Be careful to work out the full interest repayment implications of any debt financing that you do.

Sources of borrowing are various, but perhaps the first choice for the self-publisher is a bank overdraft. This arrangement can be a good way to complement working capital because it is a relatively cheap way to borrow. Usually the bank will require some security to set against the overdraft facility. This could be a mortgage, or a guarantee by a third party.

You can also take out a bank loan for a fixed period of time. These are usually restricted to a specific purpose, however, and repayment is often required on a fixed time scale.

Another way of borrowing is through hire purchase agreements. These tend to be more expensive than bank finance, but can be important for equipment purchases like cameras and accessories. The finance house remains the legal owner of the equipment until you have paid it off, but once you have paid the deposit you can start using it. In addition you can enter the asset value for capital allowance purposes (see tax section below).

Business practices

In general it is sensible to follow certain basic business practices, no matter how small your business may be.

It is a good idea, therefore, to keep business and personal transactions separate and to open a business bank account. Bank all business receipts quickly, and pay all expenses by cheque unless they are small enough to come out of petty cash. Make sure you keep a record of all receipts and payments, and organise your records carefully.

Try to keep your records as up to date as possible by instituting a systematic recording and accounting procedure.

Pay attention to the capital you need at any stage in the business. Make sure you retain enough profit to supplement your working capital needed to cope with inflationary pressures, and finance growth. And try not to keep huge stocks over a long period, because they represent money standing idle.

If you don't know how to do something connected with running your business, seek professional advice. It will save you trouble and money in the long run.

Invoicing and terms

An important key to your business success is the terms under which you trade with your customers. It is critical that you receive money from the products you sell and that this arrives in your bank account when you expect it to.

During your business planning you should have taken a view as to how long you are prepared to wait between investing money to produce what you are self-publishing, and the time when money starts coming back in the form of receipts for sales. Minimising this time is very much to your advantage because you are either paying interest on money borrowed to finance your production, or you are losing potential interest on the money you yourself put into the business.

The other main way in which your money can be tied into the business with no return is when you extend credit to your customers. You extend credit as soon as you invoice a buyer and give them time in which to pay you. This is a very common business practice of course, but it can lead the unwary into trouble.

For example, if you are just starting up in business and want to do all you can to encourage as many buyers as possible to take your product, you may give all of them credit. But you have already paid for your product and it is no longer available to be sold if a creditor is holding it, so depending on your cash flow you will want payment within a reasonable time. It can also be very time consuming trying to collect bad debt from creditors who appear unwilling to pay.

It is crucial, therefore to keep track of any invoices that are outstanding. It is also important to make plain the terms under which you extend credit *before* it is extended. Thus when invoicing you should specify a "pay by" date, otherwise traders will either assume "usual" times, or worse, not bother until pressed for payment.

The time you allow from delivery should be reasonable. For example, many small retailers work on 30 days credit, whereas public institutions like local councils may take three months as the norm for paying invoices.

A piece of advice I was given when I started selling postcards was to get cash on delivery. I was keen to do this to avoid potential problems with non-payers, though the method did not go down well with some of my customers, who expected "usual terms" to apply. However, I did find that for small transactions with small customers cash on delivery was best. Cash on delivery also has the advantage of cutting collection costs, and in any event it is also a sound strategy for initial deliveries.

With larger accounts I was prepared to trust my judgement over who would trade fairly. Experience soon showed me which of my customers were good payers and which weren't. Luckily, most paid in the end. I was caught out on one or two occasions, but on the whole I found retailers were honest people.

It does pay to be flexible over the longer term, when you have discovered who are the good, bad or "never" payers. You should only extend credit on an open account if you have a lot of faith in the buyer and reliable references to confirm your judgement. A distribution company might fall into this category, for example.

Bad debts

Whatever the payment terms you decide on, always state them clearly, and follow up on late payers. You are losing money if you do not, and subsidising your customer's business into the bargain.

However, do not jump into legal action immediately an invoice becomes due. After all it just may be an oversight. Also, as a small businessperson yourself, it is can be costly and time consuming to go through a legal process.

So take assertive action first. Send out an invoice reminder pointing out in a courteous manner that payment is now due. Alternatively you can telephone the person responsible for paying invoices and ask when you can expect to be paid. If at all possible it is usually better to use courtesy, persistence and rely on the buyer's sense of guilt to secure payment, rather than threatening them.

As mentioned above the best method for small scale customers is getting cash on delivery, but if you are dealing with larger companies who have a lot of financial muscle you may have to live with their terms rather than your own. You can afford to do this if you get some benefit, like a big order. However just because a firm is big, and could pay you easily, don't think it follows they will. I waited nearly a year, sending many demanding letters, before I got paid by one of the largest companies in the area.

If your persistence does not pay off you will have to consider legal action to recover your debt. Do not hold back on this by thinking that you might get paid next week. If a customer has ignored you thus far it is unlikely that you will get paid by waiting further. Most firms will pay within the terms of your invoicing procedures, or shortly after. Those that don't should be dealt with once you have reached your time limit for late payment.

Before taking legal action you can try to ascertain why the debt has not been paid. If the reason is cash flow problems you could negotiate a schedule of payments by instalments, or you could ask for post-dated cheques, or a promissory note saying when the debt will be paid. In any of these cases you could also ask for interest on the amount owed to be built into the repayments.

If you get no satisfaction this way, or decide not to find out why the debt is not being paid, then your next step could be to send a letter threatening legal action. This often has the desired effect of getting the payment without actually going to court. Make sure your letter is convincing. The debtor has to believe you will carry out your threat unless you receive satisfaction.

If this last stage still doesn't work, then you have the choice of writing off the debt or taking legal action.

Take legal action as soon as possible after it becomes apparent to you that your customer has no intention of paying you. But bear in mind that costs are involved and that you may still not recover your money, especially if your customer goes bankrupt. Ask for advice on the most appropriate course of legal action, as this will depend on the circumstances. The Citizens' Advice Bureau can be very helpful, and you should look into the small claims court procedures to see whether they apply to you.

Finally if you are forced to write off bad debt, keep a record of it as you may be able to deduct it from income and thereby not pay tax on it. You can get further advice from your accountant or the Inland Revenue.

Tax matters

The first thing you should do when you start trading, as a self-publisher or as a freelance, is inform the Inland Revenue and send your local inspector of taxes a form 41G. The form can be found currently in the booklet IR28, entitled "Starting in Business". However as the Inland

Revenue brings out new or changed information periodically do check all those publications likely to be relevant or new.

You should also inform your local office of the Department of Social Security, who need to know for National Insurance contribution purposes.

You will need to start record books and keep proper accounts. Unless your turnover exceeds a specific amount you do not need to register for Value Added Tax (and therefore do not need to invoice for VAT). But if your turnover is large and above the amount set for VAT purposes you must register. However, even if your turnover is below the amount specified you can register if you are eligible to do so. VAT is dealt with in more detail later in this chapter.

You are allowed to choose the date when your accounts are made up for tax purposes. Once chosen, your accounts usually should be made up on that date each year. Income tax is normally assessed for the year ending 5 April, but you can choose a different date for your business accounts if you wish.

There are special rules governing tax when you first start your business. For the first income tax year an assessment is made on the profits from when you started the business up to April 5. If you make up your accounts to a later date a proportion is taken. In the next income tax year an assessment is based on the first twelve months' profits. In the third income tax year the assessment is based on the twelve months ending on the usual accounting date in the preceding tax year. If no year fits then the assessment is based on the profits of the first twelve months of trading.

Preparing the accounts

You are responsible for the accuracy of your accounts and for correctly declaring the amount of profit. However you can employ an accountant to draw up the accounts for you, based on information given by you. You are not obliged to engage an accountant, but if you do their fees can be claimed against tax.

For tax purposes your accounts will usually be in two parts. The first is the "profit and loss account" which provides a summary of the trading transactions throughout the year. The second is the "balance sheet" which sets out the assets and the liabilities of the business at the end of the tax year.

Both these accounts depend on full and accurate records, and it is in your interest to maintain these from the moment you begin trading.

If you cannot give the tax inspector an accurate statement of your profits you will be charged tax on an estimate of your profits, which could well be higher than they actually are. If you have an accountant, accurate book-keeping will help him or her and mean less time spent on drawing your accounts up, and this in turn will keep the accountant's fee down.

In general you should keep figures for: your business takings; expenditure, such as stock bought for resale, rent, lighting, heating, insurance, repairs to premises and fixtures and fittings, motor vehicle running expenses, stationery, postage and telephone; private money introduced into the business; cash taken from the business for your own use; cheques drawn on the business for private use; the market value of goods taken from the business for your own use; amounts owed to you by customers at the accounting date; amounts owed by you to suppliers at the accounting date.

The "profit and loss" account is made up by setting total income against total allowable expenditure and calculating the difference. If the figure is positive – that is, your income is greater than your expenditure – you have made a profit which is taxable. If the figure is negative you have made a loss.

Allowances

There are many rules for working out the profits of your business for income tax purposes. The two most important ones are that capital expenditure is not an allowable deduction, and that the only expenses which are deductible are those incurred wholly and exclusively for the purpose of the business.

For the purposes of income tax a distinction is drawn between capital and revenue expenditure. In general terms, expenditure is capital when its value is not used up in a tax year, and is revenue when it recurs regularly year by year. For the self-publisher this means that cameras, accessories and other equipment such as a business computer is a capital expenditure, and thus cannot be set against income tax. Revenue expenditure would cover items such as film and processing, advertising, stationery and the like.

However the cost of capital equipment can attract special allowances, called capital allowances. These reduce the income on which tax is chargeable. What kinds of equipment attract these allowances is not always straightforward, and further information is available from your local tax office. It is worth checking whether you can claim these.

PROFIT AND LOSS ACCOUNT

	This Month	Year to Date
INCOME		
Sales		
Commissions		
Other		
Total **[1]**		
EXPENSES		
Marketing		
Sales costs (e.g. delivery)		
Film		
Processing		
Production costs		
Packaging		
Other		
Total **[2]**		
GROSS PROFIT = **[1] - [2] = [3]**		
OVERHEADS		
Salary		
Lighting		
Heating		
Telephone		
Office materials		
Vehicle costs		
Professional fees (e.g. accountant)		
Bank interest		
Bad debts		
Other		
Total **[4]**		
NET PROFIT =		

Sample profit and loss account; see text for further details.
It is important for tax and cash flow reasons to maintain basic accounting records.

If you start your self-publishing business with cameras and other equipment which you already own, then you can claim for these, but not at their original cost. The allowance will be based on their value at the date you brought them into the business.

Further information on the rules governing capital allowances, for example on short life assets like computers, is available from your local tax office.

To make a claim you will need to supply information on what you have bought, the date you bought it, the cost, whether you use it only for business purposes, or whether you use it for private purposes too. If the latter is the case you need to work out the proportion of business use. But if you do claim for something and you later want to sell it, then you need to supply information on what you have sold, the date you sold it and how much you received for it, either in cash or part exchange.

Once you have these figures you work out the value of equipment in the business at the end of each tax year (the pool), and make a claim as a separate item on your tax return. The claim should not be part of the overall expenditure figure. What you can claim is called a writing down allowance, and this is a percentage of the value of the pool. This figure is then deducted from the pool which forms the basis for the pool in the following tax year, when you repeat the process again.

Cars bought for business purposes attract capital allowances, but are treated separately to other equipment.

Where you use your car for both business and private purposes, an appropriate division between capital allowances and running expenses has to be made. The tax inspector will need information about business and total mileage so this can be calculated. Note that journeys to and from a regular place of work are not treated as an allowable business expense but as private expenditure.

Also in the category of private expenses are things like food, clothing, medical treatment, premiums on personal insurance policies and national insurance contributions.

Losses

If you make a loss you can do four main things.

First you can set the loss against future profits from the same business, starting with the earliest year in which you record a profit. You are allowed six years from the year in which you made a loss to tell the tax inspector you want to do this.

Second, you can claim relief for the same income tax year as the year of the loss. So, if you have another job where you pay income tax, then you can set the loss against it. The loss, normally of your accounting year, can be deducted from your other income in the income year in which your accounting year ends. You are allowed two years from the end of the income tax year in which your accounting year of loss ends to tell the tax inspector that you want to claim this relief.

Third, you can claim relief for the income tax year following the loss. This is similar to the second point above except that the loss is deducted from the following years income. You have three years in which to inform the tax inspector that you wish to do this.

Fourth, you can claim relief for the three years prior to the year in which you make the loss, starting with the earliest year. You can only do this, however, if the loss occurs within the first four income tax years of your business. You are allowed two years from the end of each income tax year of loss to make this claim.

Finally, if you decide to cease trading as a self-publisher or to close your freelance business, the assessment for income tax for the year in which you stop is based on the profits from the beginning of the income tax year to the date of cessation. The Inland Revenue can then also revise the assessment for the two income tax years before the income tax year in which you cease trading, to amounts based on the actual profits, for income tax purposes, of those years.

Assets and liabilities

The balance sheet consists of a statement about the assets your business has, and its liabilities.

Assets are items of value to a business, and they have a value to the future of the business. Accountants distinguish between current and fixed assets. Current assets are those that would not normally keep their current form for more than a year. They include trading stock, such as your actual products, raw materials, debtors and cash. Fixed assets are those that have a life expectancy of more than a year, and include equipment and motor cars.

Liabilities are amounts owed by the business. They are long-term if they are not required to be met within one year, whereas if they fall due within the year they are current liabilities. Your assets therefore, can be viewed as productive resources, or a means of meeting liabilities. You should keep enough assets to meet current liabilities. If you don't, your business could run into difficulties. Your working capital is the difference between your current assets and your current liabilities.

At the end of your accounting period you can assess your assets by a stock take which values product stock, raw materials and partly completed work. Consumables such as film should be valued at their cost to you. Stocks of finished products for resale and other work in progress should usually be valued at their cost to you. Other assets are amounts owed to your business, by customers for example.

You also need to assess your liabilities, that is the amounts you owe to suppliers, such as printers etc.

National Insurance

If you are self-employed you normally have to pay weekly, flat rate Class 2 National Insurance contributions plus earnings-related Class 4 contributions on profits between certain limits. If you have other paid employment you will be liable to pay class 1 contributions as well. However there is a maximum liability in this case and you may be able to defer payment of Class 2 and 4 contributions in certain circumstances. Applications for deferment should normally be made before the tax year commences.

Class 2 contributions are collected by the Department of Social Security. Class 4 contributions are normally calculated, assessed and collected by the Inland Revenue at the same time as the income tax on your business profits.

When working out your total income you can deduct one half of the finally settled amount of Class 4 contributions you are liable to pay for that year of assessment.

Remember to consult your tax office about National Insurance, as the rules can change from time to time.

VAT

The other tax you have to give some thought to is Value Added Tax. You are required to register for VAT if your taxable turnover exceeds certain limits, but if you are just starting out in business as a self-publisher this limit is very unlikely to apply to you.

At the time of writing the threshold for VAT registration was £46,000; you should check the current figure when necessary. If your business does not reach the threshold you can still apply to register, although Customs and Excise are at liberty to refuse your application. If you can demonstrate that you would be at a trading disadvantage by not being registered, then your application would be more likely to stand a chance of succeeding.

The obvious advantages of being VAT registered are that you can claim the VAT back on your materials and equipment costs. Since, at the time of writing, VAT is 17.5% in the UK, this could be a considerable saving.

Once registered, your book-keeping must incorporate VAT, and returns are usually made every quarter. You must charge VAT on everything you sell, although some items like books are zero-rated at the time of writing. Your invoices must show your VAT registration number, and full details of the VAT charged, separate from other costs.

At the end of each accounting period you have to complete a VAT return, listing your business output and showing the total value and the amount of VAT charged. Against this you can set VAT on your purchases. If the value of the VAT paid to you exceeds the VAT you have paid on your purchases, then you must pay the difference to the Customs and Excise. If, however, you have paid more VAT on legitimate business expenses than you have received on sales etc., you can claim the difference from the Customs and Excise.

Customs and Excise have the power to keep records and documents for a maximum of six years from the end of your accounting period.

If you want to know more about VAT, or have any doubts about it, then consult your accountant or local VAT office.

One reason you may have for wanting to register for VAT is because it gives the impression of a professional, large-scale business. However, if you are running a small venture the extra paperwork and time required to charge and claim VAT may not be worthwhile. Your professional image can be built up in other ways.

Copyright

When you take a photograph you have created something. In order to prevent someone else from simply copying your picture and using it as their own it is subject to copyright. Copyright includes protection for all "artistic works", so if you have self-published using non-commercial processes these are protected by copyright too.

Copyright protects the expression of ideas, not the idea itself. So it will not necessarily protect your concept, only your finished work. What copyright certainly protects is the reproduction of your image or product as a whole. Your copyright would be infringed if a person making use of your idea also reproduces your whole image or a "substantial part" of it, though what constitutes a substantial part may be difficult to determine.

In the UK all you have to do is create a work for it to be automatically covered by copyright, provided the work is original. You do not have to assert your claim to copyright, but it is usual and advisable to put the copyright symbol – © – on your work, along with your name and the date. In some countries abroad you are required to do this and may also be required to register the work first.

Copyright protection extends to other countries which have reciprocal copyright arrangements with the UK. In most the length of time that copyright extends is the creator's lifetime plus 50—70 years. If you are selling posters, cards or books abroad it is worthwhile finding out the relevant regulations for the countries concerned.

Copyright invariably belongs to the "author" of the work; that is, you, as creator. So you may do with it as you wish, including assigning it to someone else. But if you are self-publishing then you will most likely want to retain the copyright at all times so that you may continue to profit from your creation.

CHAPTER CHECKLIST

● Have you considered the business side of self-publishing before getting started?

● Have you decided on what kind of business structure you are going to adopt?

● Have you prepared a business plan?

● Have you instituted a good filing and information retrieval system?

● Have you decided on what records you should keep?

● Have you considered getting a computer system to generate statements, invoices, reminders and the like?

● Have you made sure you are keeping a record of all expenses that are claimable against tax?

● Have you prepared a cash flow budget?

● Have you considered how you will finance your self-publishing business (seed capital), and run it (working capital)?

● Have you thought through your procedures for invoicing and collection of debt?

● Have you informed the Inland Revenue that you are starting a business?

● Are you making sure that your book-keeping is accurate and up to date?

● Have you asserted copyright on your products, and are you aware the latest copyright legislation?

● Have you reviewed your business performance?

Further Reading

Art, Design and Craft: A Manual for Business Success
J. Crowe & J. Stokes.
Edward Arnold. ISBN 0-7131-7514-1.

The Barclays Guide to Buying and Selling for the Small Business
J.S. Gammon.
Blackwell. ISBN 0-631-17528-8.

The Gum Bichromate Book
David Scopick.
Focal Press. ISBN 0-240-80073-7.

Inspired Selling
J.T. Auer.
Kogan Page. ISBN 0-7494-0485-X.

Marketing Management, Analysis, Planning, Implementation and Control
Philip Kotler.
Prentice-Hall International. ISBN 0-13-556267-8.

Photographic Possibilities
"The expressive use of ideas, materials and processes."
Robert Hirsch.
Focal Press. ISBN 0-240-80047-8.

Publishing Photography
"A practical guide for photographers interested in publishing their work in book form."
Dewi Lewis & Alan Ward.
Cornerhouse Publications. ISBN 0-948797-81-9.

Successful Marketing in a Week
E. Davies & B.J. Davies.
British Institute of Management/Hodder & Stoughton.

Index

Accounting 20, 121-123, 129-134
Advertising 83-84

Bad debts 127-128
Book-keeping 17, 119, 121-123,
    125-126, 130
Books 13, 28-30, 43, 46, 52-53, 61,
    66, 82, 86
Business plans 44, 118

Camera bags 36
Cameras 34
    —formats 30, 34, 37, 38
Cash flow forecasting 123-124
Colour separations 49-50, 53
Computers 119-121
Contracts 86, 112, 117
Copyright 135-136
Craft fairs 19, 113-114
Cromalins 51, 52, 56

Discounts 79, 89-90, 99-100
Distribution 13, 16, 82-83, 86, 90
Dot gain 53, 55, 56
Duotone printing 50, 54

Exhibitions 19, 110-111, 112

Film 31-33
    —formats 31-32, 38
    —processing 38, 81
Filters 36
Finance 14, 44-45, 124-125
Focusing 36-38
Frames 45, 92, 106

Galleries 19, 109, 110-113

Greetings cards 28, 67, 78, 82

Income tax 17, 20, 121, 128-130,
    132-133
    —allowances 122, 130-132
Invoicing 17, 82, 126-127

Lenses 33-34
Light meters 34-35
Limited companies 117-118

Market research 23, 24, 42-43, 44,
    45-46, 61-66, 69, 87
Mark-ups 78, 89

National Insurance 129, 134

Packaging 90-92
Paper 55, 56, 57
Partnerships 117
Petty cash 123
Postcards 12 *passim*
    —reverse 15, 25
Posters 23, 26-28, 38, 46, 61, 66,
    82, 91, 92
Pricing 19, 43, 44, 78-81, 88-90,
    112
Printing 16, 18, 43, 46-58
Prints
    —fine art 19, 104-109
    —gum bichromate 104, 107
    —image transfer 104, 108
    —limited edition 106
    —photographic 50-51, 104,
    105-106
    —silk screen 108-109
Process cameras 48-49

Product range 11, 17, 22-23, 24, 26, 45, 66, 67-69, 95

Production values 15, 18, 66, 68, 79-80, 105

Promotion 16, 81-82, 109-110

Proofing 51-55, 56

Retail outlets 16, 18, 45-46, 63-64, 83, 89

Samples 95

Sales techniques 92-102

Scanning 48, 49-50

Screens 48, 55-56

Self-employment 116-117, 134

Tripods 35-36

VAT 78-79, 129, 134-135